Contemporary Roman Catholicism Crises and Challenges

Rosemary Radford Ruether

Sheed & Ward

Sheed & Ward TM is a service of National Catholic Reporter Publishing, Inc.

Library of Congress Catalog Card Number: 86-63366

ISBN: 0-934134-98-7

Published by:

Sheed & Ward
115 E. Armour Blvd. P.O. Box 414292
Kansas City, MO 64141-0281

To order, call: (800) 821-7926

Contents

*This book is dedicated to
Sister Marjorie Tuite,
in life and death a witness
against injustice in the Church
and in American Society.*

Introduction

Being a Catholic in the United States of America has never been an easy experience. American Catholics belong to a nation which was vehemently anti-Catholic in its English Protestant foundations and remained so until fairly recently. This environment has shaped American Catholicism in contradictory ways. On the one hand, the experience of living in a society where the dominant culture was hostile to their religious faith made American Catholics defensive, re-enforcing the general post-Reformation Catholic tendencies to withdraw into a self-enclosed fortress dedicated to preserving its scorned perception of truth against the "errors of the modern world." Catholic education until the 1960's tended to look at all Western culture since the thirteenth century as one long decline from a glorious past where Catholic truth and public culture were one. Catholic education was seen as a process of fortification against a surrounding world led astray by a "syllabus of errors," which included virtually every going idea since the Reformation.[1] All philosophy since the seventeenth century and most social and historical sciences were included in these errors.

On the other hand, Catholics in America have been eager Americanizers. They have sought to prove their loyalty to their country against a Protestant culture suspicious that a Catholic could not be a "good American." Catholics rallied to the revolutionary cause in the 1770's. Charles Carroll, scion of a leading Maryland Catholic family, led this identification of Catholics and patriotism. Elected as a delegate from Maryland to the Continental Congress, he was a signer of the Declaration of Independence.[2]

Catholics had reason to identify with the revolutionary cause. The break with the English crown and its established church also dissolved the English penal laws which had made American Catholics second-class citizens politically, professionally and socially.

The American Revolution did not dissolve bigotry against Catholics, and Protestant anti-Catholicism was renewed in the second half of the nineteenth century when the avalanche of new immigrants from Catholic cultures began to threaten Anglo-Saxon Protestant hegemony. But official Catholicism continued to seek to prove its compatibility with American citizenship. This often led to a twofold boosterism, a super-patriotism both as Americans and as Catholics. This author can still vividly remember being told by grade school nuns that we should see ourselves as doubly blessed, since we belonged both to the best religion in the world and the best nation in the world. The providential hand of God was seen behind both of these preeminences. God had both founded our religion and had elected our nation to "lead the world." This anxious effort to prove themselves 200% all-American left Catholics little room to be critical of American foreign policy in the period prior to the 1960's.

For most Catholics, loyalty both to their church and to their country created a certain split-mindedness due to an effort to reside politically in one system of values and religiously in another. Politically, Catholics as Americans believed in democracy, egalitarian individualism, toleration of pluralism, separation of church and state. Religiously, they adhered to a church that was officially absolutist and monolithic and where "error had no rights."

A few Catholic intellectuals and church leaders sought a more creative synthesis of the two systems of values. John Carroll, the first American bishop, in the early years of his episcopacy was friendly to the idea that a new kind of Catholicism should emerge here, shaped by the American experience. Self-governing, freed from dependency on foreign control, English or Roman, American

Catholicism could be democratized. Bishops would be elected by their clergy and local churches governed in their temporal affairs by lay trustees elected by the parish. American Catholicism would lead the way for the global church in showing the good fruits of the union of Catholicism and the principles of the Enlightenment.[3]

But these early efforts to articulate a Catholicism shaped by American revolutionary values were soon overwhelmed by the influx of a European baroque Catholicism which was moving in the opposite direction. For this European Catholicism, centered in a triumphalistic papacy, the answer to the Enlightenment was increased institutional monarchism and ideological infallibilism. American democratic values were seen as a threat to authority in a church in which authority was the essence of Catholicism. This identification of Catholicism with monolithic authoritarianism was expressed by a directive issued in 1907 that signaled the demise of earlier traditions of parish self-government:

> The church is not a republic or democracy, but a monarchy... all her authority is from above and rests in her Hierarchy; while the faithful of the laity... have absolutely no right whatever to rule and govern.[4]

In the late nineteenth century progressive bishops such as John Ireland, and intellectuals such as Orestes Brownson and Isaac Hecker, founder of the American community, the Paulist Fathers, sought to articulate a new reconciliation of Catholicism and liberal values. These values included the acceptance of separation of church and state and religious pluralism, an active role of the laity in shaping the mission of the church and the support of movements for social justice in the larger society, particularly the rights of labor.[5] But these efforts were stifled by the Vatican condemnation of a vaguely defined heresy called "Americanism" in 1897. Its full-scale death and burial followed the purges of any progressive ideas in American Catholic seminaries and colleges in response to the condemnation of modernism in 1907. These purges virtually destroyed nascent American Catholic intellectual life for a generation.[6]

The debate about Americanism was complicated by the ethnic pluralism of the American Catholic church. For many immigrant

Catholics their religion was the way to keep their distinctive culture and language. Their parish church was the community center of a transplanted ethnic enclave. For them, Americanization meant losing their distinctive French, Polish, Italian or Hispanic cultural and religious heritage, and assimilating both into an English-speaking society and an Irish-dominated church which were foreign, not only to their ethnic but to their religious traditions. Yet many of these non-Irish Catholicisms brought traditions of lay participation in church government. Americanization for them often meant the loss of these democratic traditions to a more monarchical system of church government.[7] The conflict over Americanization and democratization in the late-nineteenth-century American Catholic church might have been different if there had been a better ability of Americanizers like Brownson to communicate across ethnic traditions.

Although visible growth was cut away, the roots of a progressive American Catholicism, nourished by liberal democratic principles, remained. New lay journals such as *Commonweal* and *Cross Currents*[8] were founded to express a new commitment to liberal Catholicism. As lay people, often outside Catholic institutions, the editors of the journals were not subject to the same clerical controls. Jesuit John Courtney Murray began again to articulate the defense of religious freedom and separation of church and state, despite official repression.[9] Not accidentally, when the document on religious liberty finally vindicated these traditions, not only for American but for world Catholicism, it was John Courtney Murray who drafted the document and American prelates who spearheaded its passage by the Second Vatican Council.

For American Catholics, the Council swept like a brush fire through a people eager to discard their inferiority complex in the larger American society. The Council had revolutionary effects throughout the global church, but the American church was particularly ready for it. Having been long identified as an immigrant, working-class church, by 1960 Catholic America was predominantly middle-class and college-educated. The Sister Formation Movement in the 1950's had been raising the level of education of religious women. In 1961 the last barriers to political achievement were broken with the election of an Irish Catholic to the presidency. John F. Kennedy represented American lay Catholics come of age. Harvard-educated, wealthy and urbane, politically liberal, Kennedy made clear that lay Catholics in politics were no pawns of the ecclesiastical hierarchy, foreign or domestic.

The election of John XXIII as Pope in 1958 and John Kennedy as president in 1961 signified for American Catholics two revolutionary transformations in their identity that were happening simultaneously. In their religious consciousness the long spell of defensiveness toward modernity was dispelled. *Aggiornamento* (bringing things up-to-date) was the new word which the Pope mandated for the church, a word whose nice Italian sound smoothed over the fact that it meant "modernization," an end to that hostility to "the modern world" that had for so long defined the stance of Catholicism. The modern ideas in philosophy, history and the social sciences, long dangerous territory for Catholics, were thrown open to their exploration with the encouragement of the highest Catholic authority, or so it seemed.

Openness to the modern world meant freedom to admit that the church had not always had it right. Freedom to admit mistakes also meant freedom to change for the better, a key Christian truth which Catholics seemed to have forgotten. In that same tumultuous decade of the 1960's American Catholics, along with other Americans, also experienced sharp blows to their nationalist triumphalism. The assumption that America meant justice and prosperity at home, freedom and democracy abroad, were questioned on both fronts. Blacks emerged in a national civil rights movement to expose centuries of racist consciousness and legal restrictions. Other non-white groups, such as Hispanics and American Indians, would follow their example. A feminist movement was reborn, apparently dormant since the winning of the vote in 1921. The exposure of structural poverty and environmental pollution gave the lie to the myth of American economic fairness and responsibility.

The myth of America the Good was also challenged in the realm of foreign policy. The Vietnamese War not only gave Americans their first taste of military defeat, but also raised a question mark over the whole pattern of American foreign policy since the Second

World War, if not before. Were our various military interventions in Asia or Latin America really about the defense of democracy, as we had been told by our government, or was this rhetoric a facade for our takeover of the defense of Western neo-colonial hegemony against the legitimate aspirations of peoples in Asia, Africa and Latin America to political and economic self-determination?

These sweeping challenges to both Catholic and American triumphalism took place in an atmosphere of resurgent optimism. Americans and Catholics felt sure of their capacity to cope with these challenges and welcomed them as an opportunity to build a better church and a better society. Or at least this appeared to be the mood in the liberal community which, for the moment, seemed to dominate public culture. There was a confident belief among such liberals in the essential good will of their fellow citizens and co-religionists, of the leaders of their country and their church. If people only saw the problem clearly, surely they would respond generously, out of a basic desire to have a truthful church and a just society.

This optimism would gradually erode in the 1970's and, still more, in the '80's, as American political leaders and the Catholic hierarchy, especially the Vatican, gave the lie to this faith in the essential good will of those in power. But in order to understand the surge of energy that took place among Americans and Catholics in this period, the rapid changes of consciousness and the surfacing of challenges and movements for change on a great variety of fronts, it is important to recall the sincerity of that moment of hope. This faith was inspired particularly by our images of those "two Johns," one a handsome, witty Irish American, the other a wise, grandfatherly Italian, both of whom radiated the sense that one could be critically truthful about the present and still release infinitely expanding hopes of a better future.

The decade of 1965-1975 was one of enormously rapid change in American Catholicism. Most obvious on the local level was the effect of liturgical renewal mandated by the Council. Although these changes were the product of a generation of work done by scholarly advocates of liturgical renewal whose thought had circulated in elite circles, for most Catholics at the base, including the clergy, these changes appeared to drop from on high. Suddenly Latin was replaced by the vernacular, familiar prayers at the end of the Mass were trimmed away, the altar was turned around so that the priest faced the people, and active participation through responses, songs and the kiss of peace was expected.

Catholics who had grown up praying their rosary during Mass, while the priest mumbled at the altar in a foreign tongue, were jolted from what they had taken to be changeless tradition. Many priests were poorly equipped to explain the rationale for the changes to the laity. I recall one elderly cleric at my family parish in La Jolla, California announcing the dropping of the reading of the Preface to the Gospel of John at the end of Mass, by glaring down from the pulpit and declaring that "as of next Sunday the Last Gospel will be suppressed," with a denunciatory look that made the people in the pew wonder uncomfortably if they had been doing something wrong all those years by reciting it.

Yet somehow most Catholics managed to figure out that the new way was an improvement. The new forms themselves conveyed the message. The laity were now to be active participants in the Mass, rather than passive spectators. The Mass was not the work of the priest by himself, but was the work of priest and people together as a community. This liturgical participation expressed the ecclesiology of the Second Vatican Council. The church is not the hierarchy, with the laity as the object of its ministry. The church is the People of God.[10] The church is essentially the community, with the clergy as its servants. All in the community are to participate in the ministry and mission of the church. Conciliarism meant that the laity participate in running the parish through parish councils, just as priests form a council around the bishop on the diocesan level and the bishops form a council with the Pope on the global level. This was called "subsidiarity." Few dared suggest it might be called "democracy" or spell out what this implied for structural changes in historic Roman Catholic polity.

A new spirit of intellectual freedom to dissent and to openly criticize church policies soon began to manifest itself, particularly in the new, lay-run newspaper, the *National Catholic Reporter,* which became the major vehicle for this new style of Catholicism. Catholic institutions, such as hospitals and colleges, began to free themselves from hierarchical control by incorporating under lay boards. A new rapprochement was developed between Catholic educational institutions and those of the rest of American society. Seeking accreditation for their degrees by the same academic associations, Catholic educational institutions now felt bound to observe the same guarantees of academic freedom.

This shift was particularly dramatic in some of the seminaries run by religious communities, such as the Jesuits. These seminaries moved into consortia with Protestant seminaries in educational clusters in areas such as Cambridge, Massachusetts, Chicago, Illinois and Berkeley, California and accepted accreditation for their theological degrees by the American Theological Association. Such Catholic seminaries are now educating their seminarians in an ecumenical context, where Protestants take the Reformation as normative, where historical-critical method in biblical studies is the established tradition and where women as well as men are preparing for ordination.

Ecumenism transformed not only the milieu of academic Catholicism but to some extent grassroots practice as well. In some areas Catholic priests joined local clergy councils with Protestant and Jewish colleagues. Pulpits were exchanged. Interfaith marriages were celebrated by ministers of both traditions together, rather than in a truncated ceremony that made the non-Catholic partner feel like a liability. Open communion occurred in more liberal parishes. Much of this ecumenical practice took place without authorization from the hierarchy. Catholics simply claimed for themselves the authority to do what seemed right.

Particularly dramatic changes occurred among American women religious. Mandated by the Second Vatican Council to renew their communities by the study of their original charisms, many took this as an invitation to a sweeping process of democratization, educational advancement of their members and diversification of their ministries. Cloister and habits were discarded. Catholic nuns were now found doing advanced degrees at major universities, such as Harvard, Yale, the University of Chicago and the University of California at Berkeley. They began to involve themselves in a variety of justice ministries for the poor of American society, to create autonomous agencies for these ministries, not controlled by the hierarchy, and even to be employed by secular institutions, such as public welfare, and to run for political office. Thousands left their orders, finding the changes insufficient, and sought new careers.[11] Some communities, such as the Immaculate Heart Sisters in Los Angeles, fell into such conflict with their archbishop over renewal that they changed to non-canonical status.[12] Some orders sought to extend their definition of membership to include married people. These changes were to cause increasing conflict between American nuns and the Vatican.

Catholics joined with other Americans in the new causes of social justice. Priests and nuns marching in demonstrations for civil rights and for peace became a common sight. Led by the Berrigan brothers, Daniel and Philip, a Catholic peace movement developed that risked long jail terms by non-violent direct action against the war in Vietnam and against nuclear armaments. Americans were treated to the surprising sight of FBI men surrounding the house of Episcopalian lawyer-theologian, William Stringfellow, to arrest Jesuit peace activist Daniel Berrigan who had gone "underground" to witness against the injustice of American justice.[13]

The links of Catholic missionaries with areas such as Central America meant that Catholics took a particularly active part in resisting American foreign policy in that area. Catholic activists were heavily involved in solidarity work for liberation movements in Nicaragua, El Salvador and Guatemala. They were prominent in the sanctuary movement that sheltered illegal aliens from those areas from arrest by the Immigration Service, shielding them from deportation, to possible torture and death, in the countries from which they had fled.[14]

This work by Catholic laity, priests and nuns in poverty, racism, Third World liberation and peace began to have its effect on some members of the American hierarchy. There was a "trickle-up" effect between grassroots activism and episcopal awareness of social justice. In 1975 the bishops of Appalachia, an exploited and poverty-ridden region of America, put together a dramatic statement on behalf of social justice.[15]

In 1980 a group of Southern bishops became involved in supporting a union boycott of a major textile company in the area, J.P. Stevens. In 1983 the American bishops as a whole issued a condemnation of nuclear war that judged such armaments incompatible with Christian principles of just war.[16] An equally daring pastoral on poverty and economic injustice began to be developed after the bishops issued their pastoral on peace.[17]

Many Americans, Catholic and Protestant, were stunned by these episcopal statements. The American Catholic hierarchy, long assumed to be the bastion of social conservativism, was suddenly releasing documents that were well to the left in the American spectrum of opinion. What could possibly have gotten into them? What lay concealed under such statements was a decade or more of grassroots involvement in these issues by Catholic people who had put themselves into situations of great risk and solidarity with the poorest in society. These activities had influenced a few bishops, who in turn had been able to persuade their colleagues of the rightness of such causes. Most of all, this meant that Christianity was being understood as implying a struggle against social sin and a quest for social justice.

But all was not smooth sailing for reform and renewal, even in the first optimistic years after the Vatican Council. The conflicts between Catholics on the left and on the right were to become sharper as conservatives gathered strength to resist these changes. A newly-militant, right-wing Catholicism organized around international movements, such as Opus Dei, and national ones, such as CUFF (Catholics United For the Faith). Conflicts erupted on the parish level around new catechetical materials for children and adults developed by those schooled in new theological and historical consciousness and educational pedagogy.

Disagreements over the new theology became conflicts over academic freedom at Catholic colleges and universities. In 1963, in the midst of the Second Vatican Council, four priest theologians who were major figures in developing the thought that was to come out of the Council, Geoffrey Diekmann, O.S.B., Hans Küng, John Courtney Murray, S.J., and Gustave Weigel, S.J., were banned by the administration of the Catholic University from speaking on campus.

To the surprise of the administration, accustomed to silent acceptance of such suppression, the ban evoked a widespread movement of protest and the organization of an alternative forum for the lectures.[18]

Undoubtedly the major area of dissent against church teaching both in theory and practice was the use of birth control. Although increasing numbers of Catholic couples had begun to practice birth control in the 1960's, they usually did so with a bad conscience and accepted a self-excommunication from the sacraments. By the mid-'60's, moral theologians such as Charles Curran and Daniel Maguire began to question the cogency of the traditional reasoning against artificial contraceptives. Priests who read their writings began to dissent and questioned applying moral sanctions to laity who confessed to using contraceptives. Lay people themselves began to write against the church's teaching from their own experience.[19] In response to this international dissent, Pope Paul VI convened a birth control commission, which included married couples, to discuss the issue. But when the commission voted for a change in the traditional teaching, the Pope was unable to accept the challenge to traditional authority that such a change represented. He opted to accept the minority report that reaffirmed the ban on artificial contraceptives.[20]

When this minority view was reaffirmed in the papal encyclical, *Humanae Vitae*, a furor erupted in the Catholic Church, especially in America. Fifty-one priests in the archdiocese of Washington, D.C. published a statement of conscience refusing to accept the encyclical. They were all suspended by Archbishop Patrick O'Boyle from exercising their ministry until they recanted. At least half would leave the priesthood.[21] But repressive measures no longer served to constrain the Catholic conscience. Most younger priests simply stopped treating contraception as a sin in confession. By 1970, 68% of Catholics were practicing banned methods of contraception and 90% dissented from the teaching of the encyclical.[22] Catholics were developing an autonomous conscience that was not willing to be informed by the teaching of the magisterium, if that teaching went counter to their own experience and moral reflection.

Reproductive rights were to be the issue that would not go away. New conflicts among Catholics emerged in the 1980's over abortion, which seemed to become the chief obsession of both the bishops and the new Pope, John Paul II. While appearing to shift the focus to defense of "life," and hence to principles analogous to those defended in the bishop's peace pastoral, in reality the anti-abortion crusade was largely a continuation of the inability of the hierarchy to accept birth control. The Pope was as vehemently opposed to birth control as to abortion. The issue of reproductive rights was linked together with the inability to accept the rights of women as autonomous persons. This was part of a panoply of sex-related issues: divorce, clerical celibacy and homosexuality. It was clear that Catholicism was burdened with an inordinate problem of sexophobia. This was to become the primary area of dissent and conflict over authority.

Pope John XXIII died in 1963, the same fateful year as the assassination of John F. Kennedy. He was followed by the cautious Paul VI, who nevertheless endorsed the basic reforms of the Council and kept the Vatican conservatives in check. However, after the brief reign of John Paul I, the Polish-bred John Paul II was elected to the papacy. It soon became evident that he was much less open to liberalization in the church and looked with grave suspicion upon both Third World liberation theologies and the liberal theologies informed by historical-critical biblical studies that were coming from Germany and Holland. Thus Catholics again saw Vatican efforts to purge and silence theologians, a thing which many had hoped was a thing of the past. Conflicts with priests and nuns whose social conscience had led them into political office and with women's religious orders over their democratized constitutions, also became major issues.

It became apparent that, just as the decade of progress of the 1960's had led to the reactionary reassertion of militarism and exploitative wealth under Ronald Reagan, the 1980's were to be an era of reaction in the church as well. Conservatives such as Jerome Hamer, O.S.A., and Cardinal Ratzinger, in power in the key positions of the Vatican Curia, seemed bent, with the blessings of the Pope, not only on reining in dissent, but on turning back the clock to a a pre-conciliar ecclesiology which saw the church vested primarily in the hierarchy.[23]

But Catholics in American and elsewhere had caught a vision of an alternative church. It would not be as easy for the Pope to silence nuns and theologians as it would be for the American president to bomb the Libyans, with the passive acquiesence of most of the American press. A new reality had been unleashed in Catholicism. No longer could the Vatican expect to end a particular debate by making a definitive pronouncement. Pronouncements that left significant constituencies dissatisfied could be expected to evoke protest, resistance and perhaps even widening dissent. As one promient lay Catholic theologian put it, instead of "Roma locuta, causa finita," it had become "Roma locuta, causa stimulata."

A new, pluralistic Catholicism was being shaped in America and throughout the world, the future of which was uncertain. Would this pluralism lead eventually to schism, such as happened in the sixteenth century? Or would the hierarchy succeed in adapting to some of it and suppressing most of it, thereby reasserting a monolithic Catholicism, slightly altered from the pre-conciliar content but with the same mentality of central authority restored? Or would an entirely new kind of Catholicism develop, permanently pluralistic, both in terms of different national styles of Catholicism and in terms of different options of thought and practice within national communities? Would a democratized Catholicism gradually emerge as the mainstream consensus, with married priests, ordained women, elected bishops, local and national synods of elected laity and clergy deliberating together and deciding on policy, such as is found in Protestant churches?

Which of these options shapes the future depends a great deal on the willingness of dissenting Catholics of the liberal left to continue to identify themselves as Catholics and to find bases in the institutional church within which they can work and worship. It is from that perspective that I wish to address the major crises and challenges to Catholicism today. I will focus this discussion upon the three major areas which I believe will shape American and global Catholicism in the next ten to twenty years—to the end of the twentieth and the beginning of the twenty-first century. How the

Catholic community responds to these three challenges will determine in large part whether Catholicism will be able to use its enormous human resources to advance truth and justice during this critical period of human history when the very survival of the planet is at stake, or whether it will lose its creative leadership in schism and repression and thus forfeit its opportunity both for its own renewal and for a positive ministry to the world.

These three challenges, which will be developed in the three following chapters of this volume, are: 1) the challenge of democratic values and human rights in the church's institutional life; 2) the demands of women for full participation in the church's ministry, and the crisis over the church's teachings on sexual morality; and 3) the challenge of Third World liberation struggles and the church's alignment with the poor in those struggles. Having developed what I see as the issues in these three broad areas of crisis and challenge to church teaching and practice, the volume will move to a concluding chapter which might be titled, "What is to be done?"

This book is addressed particularly to liberal-left Catholics, like myself, who are deeply perplexed about whether they can continue to identify with this church or find a positive base from which to work for change within it. In the final chapter I will give some reasons why it is important for such Catholics of the left to take seriously our responsibility for the future of the institutional Roman Catholic Church. I will also suggest how it might be possible to find continued bases for creative thought and action in the Catholic community during a period in the life of our church and of our nation when reactionary retrenchment against reform and renewal is common.

CHAPTER 1
THE CHALLENGES OF
LIBERALISM

Conflicts between church and state are as old as the history of Christianity. The Christian church was shaped for its first three centuries by sporadic persecution by the pagan Roman imperial state which regarded the spread of this unauthorized sect as a threat to the divine origins of the *Pax Romana*. Constantine ended this phase of church-state relations and inaugurated a second phase which can be said to have lasted roughly to the French Revolution, although the disintegration of Christendom began before that date and its remnants survive today. This second phase of church-state relations was characterized by the integration of church and state in one public legal order of society. However, from the late fourth century, when Ambrose, the bishop of Milan, barred the emperor Theodosius from communion until he bowed to the church's decree,[1] two conflicting models of church-state relations have divided Western Christendom, the theocratic model and the statist model.

In the theocratic model, the temporal power of the state bows to the superior authority of the church. Primary authority is seen as given by God through Christ to the church and especially, in the Roman Catholic tradition, to the Pope, the bishop of Rome, as Vicar of Christ. The Pope and the bishops not only have supremacy over the church in the making of doctrine and jurisdiction over ecclesiastical affairs, but they also dictate the faith and moral codes which are to be adhered to by all citizens of the society. Kings and princes are not to be seen as holding priestly power, but rather, as Christian laymen, they accept the doctrinal and moral teachings of the church from the ecclesiastical hierarchy and administer the temporal realm under the tutelage of the church. In this system, the state is the "temporal arm" of the church. Heretics condemned by the church are handed over to the state for execution.

In the statist model, by contrast, the emperor is seen as supreme over church and state as one sacred unity. The church is an arm of the state. Bishops are to be appointed by the head of the state, and the temporalities of the church are to be administered by the state. Although the church, assembled in councils of bishops, makes decisions about doctrine, it does so under the patronage of the emperor who calls the Council and foots the bill for the bishops' travel. The emperor is seen as a sacred person who sums up priestly as well as kingly power, although the prophetic role is still reserved for the church, especially for the monastic community. This view came to be the predominant one in Eastern Orthodox Christianity.[2]

However, modified versions of the statist view were also held by Western Christian kings, beginning with Charlemagne's restitution of the Holy Roman Empire. Throughout the Middle Ages those who claimed the title of Western Holy Roman Emperor, and then the emerging national kings of England, France and Spain, fought with the papacy about the jurisdiction over the church in their territories.[3] The Reformation saw the triumph of a nationalist type of statism. In Protestant lands the papal claims of jurisdiction were rebuffed by handing over the temporal control of the church to the national kings and princes. As church lands were confiscated, the clergy became the stipendiaries of the state. But even in Spain and France, the champions of the Catholic counter-Reformation, the Pope remained spiritual head of the church only by ceding key elements of ecclesiastical jurisdiction, such as the appointment of bishops, to the Catholic kings.

In the sixteenth to eighteenth centuries, these Catholic monarchs enforced Catholic confessionalism in their territories. Protestantism was banned, and only Catholics could be members of their states. The clergy were a privileged caste with their own ecclesiastical courts. Their property was exempt from taxation. The Catholic Church controlled education, marriage and care of the sick. But the price the church paid for these Catholic confessional states was its captivity to the national monarchs. The Pope's word might still be final on doctrinal matters, but the enforcement of his will, and even the protection of the Papal States, the central portion of Italy which the Pope ruled as his private patrimony, was dependent on the support of the armies of these Catholic monarchs. Papal absolutism conceded to and supported royal absolutism. Only by recognizing the political weakness of the Pope, in spite of his claims to spiritual power, can one understand the Vatican's response to the French Revolution and to liberalism.

Liberal ideas, such as freedom of thought and its public communication, separation of church and state, abolition of class hierarchy in favor of equal civil status of all (male propertied) citizens, freedom of assembly and popular sovereignty, had been circulating among the intelligentsia, including the clergy, in the eighteenth century, especially in France. But the French Revolution translated all this into political reality for the Catholic Church. The American Revolution did not have the same impact, since it was seen as taking place in a distant, Protestant area. But France was a different matter. France was the "eldest daughter of the church," the heartland of Catholic Europe.

In 1789 Louis XVI was forced to summon the parliament, the Estates General, for the first time in one hundred and seventy-five years. The bourgeois, or third estate, quickly took control, with the support of the first estate, or the clergy, against the nobility. Sweeping reforms were proposed for the church as well as for the organization of the state. The plan for the reform of the church that emerged from the National Assembly was a reflection of both liberal and Gallican principles. Gallicanism referred to the assumption held by most Frenchmen, lay as well as clergy, that the French church, although it was in communion with the Pope, administered its own ecclesiastical affairs under the French king.

The Civil Constitution of the Clergy, drawn up by a committee of the National Assembly, chaired by a French bishop, would have integrated the French church into a democratized French state administration. Dioceses were to coincide with civil departments of state. The bishops and the clergy would be elected by the electorate of each of these civil departments. The results of these elections would be reported to the Pope, but the Pope would have no authority to intervene in these matters of church administration.[4] This administrative autonomy of the French church was, in itself, not a new idea; rather it simply systematized what had long been taken for granted by French churchmen and by the French king and his administrators.

For the Pope, the Civil Constitution of the Clergy was intolerable. Not only did it bring out into the open what had been masked under the alliance of throne and altar—the impotency of the papacy in the administration of national churches—but it also transferred the key decisions about bishops and clergy from the hierarchical to the popular level. But so accustomed was the Pope to ceding to the French king in matters of local church administration, that it was eight months before he condemned it. By this time the King had approved it and directed all the clergy to take an oath of allegiance to it. The Pope's condemnation split the French church in half. Roughly fifty percent, mostly the lower clergy, supported it, while another fifty percent, including most of the bishops, opposed it.

However, this moderate, reformist phase of the French Revolution, under the king and National Assembly, quickly gave way to more radical stages. The king was executed; the nobility and the non-juror clergy became persecuted enemies of the revolutionary state. Christianity was abolished altogether, and a philosophical state cult of "Reason" was established. The trauma of this Reign of Terror hardened conservatives throughout Europe against liberalism. Democratic principles were seen as leading to a violent dismantling of the social fabric of church and society, not to peaceful amelioration.

Napoleon brought to an end this conflict between revolutionary state and persecuted churchmen. In the Concordat of 1801, which Napoleon signed with Pope Pius VII, Catholicism was reestablished as the protected religion of the French state. All bishops, jurors and non-jurors alike, were to resign and be reappointed by Napoleon, with the final approval of the Holy See. Since church property confiscated at the Revolution was not restored, the clergy were to become state stipendiaries.[5] In Napoleon's settlement with the Pope, the democratization of the French church of the Civil Constitution of the Clergy was abolished, but the essential Gallicanism remained. This fact must be borne in mind in order to understand the alliance of liberals and ultramontanes in Europe, especially France, in the 1830's to 1860's.

For French Catholic conservatives in the first decades of the nineteenth century, the key to social stability was restoration of hierarchical authority, lodged in the twin absolute monarchies of king and Pope. It was Felicité de Lamennais who originally was allied with these traditionalists, who recognized that this system actually made the church the political captive of the French state. He sought to ally the papacy with liberal principles in order to free the church from this control by the state. He tried to convert the Pope and church leadership to the principles of separation of church and state, and freedom of education, press and religion, in order to free the French Catholic Church from its encapsulation by the French bureaucratic apparatus of control. By endorsing these liberal principles, the church could emerge as an autonomous, international organization which had regained control over its own institutional life. He looked to the Pope to become the head of this liberated church, which would, in turn, become a beacon light for the renewal of European society on democratic principles.'

But de Lamennais' hopes were soon dashed to the ground. Gregory XVI condemned de Lamennais, who soon after left the church to become an embittered radical democrat. Although the Pope was pleased with de Lamennais' ultramontane principles of restored papal jurisdiction over national episcopacies, he conceived of this happening through concordats with Catholic monarchs, not within democratic societies. For him, ecclesiastical and social hierarchy were indispensable principles of social order. If political monarchy was put in question, papal monarchy would soon follow. He wanted authoritarian Catholic states that would maintain the privileged status of the Catholic Church. He also wanted them to defend the temporal power of the Pope in the papal states, which was, at that time, being threatened by the Italian *risorgimento*, the movement led by Italian liberals and nationalists for national unity. Such a unification of Italy as a modern nation-state could not happen without confiscating the papal states which divided the northern from the southern third of Italy.

The papal struggle against liberalism through the nineteenth century must be seen as fundamentally conditioned by this Italian context. For the Pope, liberalism meant, most immediately, the dismantling of the papal states in order to create an Italian secular nation independent of the Pope. The Pope would be reduced to a property-less status. It was simply assumed by the popes of the period that the papacy could not survive as an institution without this material base.

This struggle was to be carried on preeminently by Pius IX, who presided over the end of the old papacy and the shaping of the new papacy that was to survive the demise of the papal states stronger than ever. Pius IX was elected in 1846 and, for two years, flirted with liberal ideas that suggested that the Pope himself might become the president of a united confederacy of Italian states. But the revolution of 1848, which forced him to flee from Rome, cured him of this brief romance with liberals. In his hands the ultramontane movement was severed from liberalism and became a tool of an emergent papacy that would regain control over its own international hierarchy, while setting its face against all the "heresies" of a Europe which, in his eyes, had become apostate from "Christian" principles. All the movements which sought to emancipate individuals and society from hierarchical control were, for him, a part of this apostasy.

In the *Syllabus of Errors* (1864), freedom of thought, education, press and religion, theories and practices of autonomy in matters of the mind and spirit, were condemned, along with the movements that would turn the political and economic apparatus of society over to popular control, such as democracy, socialism and communism. The last section of the *Syllabus* specifically repudiated freedom of religion and defended the confessional Catholic state against legal rights granted other religious groups (i.e. Protestants) or the free discussion of ideas generally. The famous concluding statement of the *Syllabus* grandly declared that it is false that "the Roman Pontiff can and should reconcile and adapt himself to progress, liberalism and modern civilization."[7]

In 1869 Pius IX summoned a general Council of the Church. It was clear in advance that the Pope intended that the Council would place supreme jurisdictional, as well as doctrinal, authority in his hands, although he did not want to appear to be promoting this himself, but to have it "emerge" by general acclamation from the bishops. This agenda was made evident when an article was published in February 1869, by a quasi-official organ of the Holy See, which contained the following statement:

> All genuine Catholics believe the Council will be quite short . . . They will receive with joy the proclamation of the dogmatic infallibility of the sovereign pontiff. It is not at all surprising that, from a feeling of proper reserve, Pius IX does not wish to take the initiative himself in proposing what seems to concern him directly, but it is

> hoped that the unanimous revelation of the Holy Spirit,
> by the mouth of the Fathers of the Ecumenical Coun-
> cil, will define it by acclamation.[8]

Behind this facade of "proper reserve," however, Pius IX and a small cadre of ultramontane infallibilists were actively engaged in controlling the Council, eliminating anti-infallibilists from attending the Council, controlling the debate, putting pressure on those who came as delegates and punishing those who proved less than whole-hearted after the Council was over. The appearance of near-unanimous acclamation (two voted against the decree in the final vote), was achieved only by more than half the eligible bishops failing to show up for the final vote.[9] This manipulation raises serious questions about the validity of Vatician I as a genuine council. The doctrine is in serious contradiction to Catholic tradition, which gave final doctrinal authority to councils which, in turn, come to a concensus based on full consultation of the theological tradition, Scripture and the faith of the people. Vatican I sought to replace this conciliar tradition with papal monarchical absolutism.

The triumph of papal absolutism in 1870 also shows, paradoxically, that one aspect of Lamennais' union of liberalism and ultramontanism was correct. The separation of church from state allowed the papacy to reemerge as the center of control over the church internationally. Freed from conflicts with national monarchs, who sought to control the church within their territories, the Pope could systematize his ancient claims to universal jurisdiction over all the episcopacies of the universal church. The price of this new autonomy of the church, as a centralized international institution, however, was the loss of direct power of the church over society. The Catholic Church in the modern world had to adapt itself from its traditions of direct legal control to indirect influence.

One way this influence was to be exercised was through the personal cult of the papacy, which imbued Catholics with a demand for unquestioning loyalty to whatever the Pope said. This personal cult of the Pope was developed under Pius IX and has characterized modern Catholicism until recently, when it began to disintegrate following the Second Vatican Council. The papal cult presents the Pope as practically God or Christ incarnate, all wise and holy. All open disagreement with the Pope is ruled out in advance. Such a view of the Pope is justly termed "papalatry." Theologically speaking, it represents not the logical defense of Christian faith, but the final apostasy from the Christian faith, which rests on the unalterable distinction between God and all fallible, finite and sinful humans and human institutions. A religion of the good news of God's forgiveness and acceptance of sinners has been translated into a religion officially incapable of repentence because it cannot admit to the possibility of error.

Pius IX and his ultramontane supporters sought to make the supreme jurisdictional and doctrinal authority of the papacy the ultimate bulwark against modern liberalism, both in the spiritual and intellectual sense of freedom of thought, discussion and communication, and in the political sense of secular, democratic forms of government. If the Catholic Church could not prevent such modern societies from coming about, it would withdraw from them and direct the "faithful" to boycott the modern world.

The day after the vote on papal infallibility was taken, war was declared between France and Prussia. Two months later the papal states had been confiscated and the new Kingdom of Italy was declared. Pius IX declared himself a "prisoner in the Vatican" and forbade Italian Catholics to support the new state. Having lost the traditional alliance of the papacy with Catholic monarchs, the Pope turned to organizing right-wing Catholic mass movements in an effort to subvert the Italian state and restore the traditional power of the Pope and the church. For more than thirty years these Catholic movements were forbidden to vote or hold office in the hated Italian liberal state. But gradually the policy of using the Catholic vote for the church's interest won out over intransigent opposition to Italian unification and parliamentary government.

The Italian liberal state of 1870-1914 was basically a bourgeois state supported by the new industrial elite. Thus Catholic movements often appealed to the largely disenfranchised rural and working classes. A Catholic Popular Party and labor unions emerged,[10] but these quickly showed their tendency to pursue agendas of social reform that had little to do with the Vatican desire to reestablish its power and privileges. So, in the 1920's, the Vatican abandoned these Catholic popular movements it had previously encouraged, to enter into a treaty and Concordat with the fascists. The 1929 Lateran agreements with Mussolini gave the church much of what it had wanted and had failed to achieve through popular Catholic, democratic movements. The long-standing "Roman question" of the confiscation of the papal states by the Italian government was settled by paying the Pope a huge indemnity of 750 million lire, and also bonds worth one billion lire (worth at that time about 19 million pounds sterling).[11]

This financial settlement, judiciously invested on the international stock market, translated the papacy into a major capitalist corporation. It is not irrelevant that the first representative of the Vatican in these negotiations with the fascists was Francesco Pacelli, brother of Eugenio Pacelli who would become Pope in 1938. Their uncle, Ernesto Pacelli, was the aggressive head of the Bank of Rome.[12] The Concordat of 1929 with Mussolini also confirmed that Catholicism was the sole religion of the Italian state. It restored Catholic instruction in primary and secondary schools, and allowed the accrediting of a Catholic university. It assured the autonomy of the Vatican state as well as the holdings of the church throughout Italy in palaces and basilicas. In effect, Italy was again made a Catholic confessional state.

Four years later, in 1933, Eugenio Pacelli, the papal nuncio to Germany, was to be the architect of a Concordat with Hitler. The Concordat with Hitler assured the Catholic Church of freedom to practice its religion, appoint clergy and conduct internal communication and publication. The German state was given the right to veto papal appointments of bishops, a concession to the state also found in the 1920 Concordat with Mussolini. Bishops and clergy were to take a loyalty oath to the German state. In turn, the state would continue to pay the subsidy for the Catholic clergy.

The Catholic Church could continue to have theological faculties at the state universities, and also to teach religion in primary, secondary and higher schools. This education should be compatible with Germany patriotism, however. The church would have the power to license these Catholic teachers of religion. Catholic pastoral care in hospitals, prisons and other such state institutions was also assured. In both the Italian and the German Concordats, Catholic clergy were forbidden to be members of or active in behalf of any political party.[13]

These two Concordats effectively tied the Catholic Church to the fascist states. As these fascist states showed themselves increasingly militarist, neo-pagan and racist in the late thirties, the Vatican was to move to increasing aloofness from them. But their policies, including the genocide of the Jews, were never openly condemned by Pacelli, now Pope Pius XII. Much has been written on this "silence of the Pope" toward fascism.[14] It has been said that he "agonized" over these evils, but kept silence because speaking out would only subject Catholics to persecution. But there is no question that a papal condemnation of fascist racism would have been enormously powerful in generating organized opposition to it. What was really at stake was the Concordats, the privileged status won for the church in the fascist states. The Pope was unwilling to jeopardize this privileged status.

It has also been suggested that the Catholic Church and fascism were natural allies because both were totalitarian societies. It is true that the Vatican trusted authoritarian regimes more than democratic ones, and certainly more than socialist ones. It saw fascism as a bulwark against socialism and communism. But this does not make Catholicism and fascism entirely compatible. In effect, each represented mutually exclusive authoritarianism.[15] Fascism was a statist totalitarianism whose ideal was the corporate state, in which all autonomous movements and organization had been eliminated. Both Hitler and Mussolini wished to subjugate the church and make it an arm of the fascist state. That they conceded some area of autonomy to the church, contrary to fascist theory, was the measure of their fear of the church's power and their desire to neutralize it.

Catholicism, in turn, had no intention of becoming simply a department of state. Ideally, it continued to hold its medieval dream of a theocratically-ordered society in which the Pope not only has supreme jurisdiction over the church hierarchy, but also is able to use the state as the "secular" arm of the church. Lacking a Catholic state, it was willing to use a fascist one to gain its own institutional autonomy, access to basic public institutions of education, prisons and hospitals, and control of matrimonial law. It conflicted with the fascist states when they threatened to encroach on its institutional territory and privileges. Thus the Catholic Church both cooperated with the fascist states and neutralized any official criticism of them, in return for maintaining its autonomy and privileges.

However, the limited immunity which the Catholic Church as an institution enjoyed in relation to the fascist state, including its extension into society in Catholic Action, provided a space where opponents of the fascist regime could organize and lay the basis for a new Italian society. Thus a Catholic resistance to fascism developed, working alongside socialists and communists. When the fascist state lay in ruins in 1945, it was the forces of the Left that emerged as major claimants to the shaping of a new Italy. But both the Catholic Church and the American occupation forces were determined to prevent this victory of the Left. The Catholic resistance that had been sheltered by the church came forth as the architects of a Christian Democratic center party to provide a new government that would ward off both the victory of a socialist-communist government and the revival of fascism.[16] This Christian Democratic party, closely associated both with the Catholic hierarchy and with Italian capitalism, has ruled Italy since 1947, although its ethical claims have been increasingly discredited. The post-war Italian government, led by the Christian Democrats, reaffirmed the basic terms of the 1929 Concordat with the Vatican.

The endorsement of Christian Democratic parties, in Italy and in other countries, was the framework for an accommodation of Catholic thought with liberalism. This was possible also because liberalism itself had lost its militant anticlerical face of the nineteenth-century revolutionary period and had become the ideology of a bourgeois establishment. A more autonomous church adjusted itself to a new relationship to the liberal establishment. The experience of American Catholicism, where the Catholic Church flourished in a pluralistic society, with no one established church, played a key role in adjusting Catholic teaching to this new reality. The Jesuit John Courtney Murray was a prime advocate for the view that accommodation to liberalism was not simply an unfortunate necessity in situations where the Catholic Church had become a minority group, while the Catholic confessional state would remain the Catholic norm. Rather, the liberal freedoms should be recognized as integral to the Christian gospel. During the Second Vatican Council, this view became official Catholic teaching.

In April 1963, Pope John XXIII issued the encyclical letter *Pacem in Terris* (Peace on Earth), addressed not only to the Catholic leadership and people but to "all men of good will." The excitement of this encyclical was captured in a headline of the *Washington Post* reporting this event, which read "THE POPE TO US."[17] To a remarkable extent the papacy under John XXIII had gained such general respect that non-Catholics could feel delighted at having an encyclical that included them. The encyclical endorsed the whole gamut of civil liberties in language that echoed the American Bill of Rights and the French *Declaration of the Rights of Man and the Citizen*. In a key statement, the encyclical states:

> Every human being is a person; that is, by nature endowed with intelligence and free will. Indeed, precisely because he (sic) is a person he has rights and obligations flowing directly and simultaneously from his

> very nature. And as these rights and obligations are
> universal and inviolable, so they cannot in any way be
> surrendered. (9)

The encyclical accepted the liberal tradition of grounding these basic rights in an egalitarian doctrine of Nature, but this is now affirmed to be based on the Christian theology of Creation, renewed in Jesus Christ.

Among the basic human rights affirmed in the encyclical are the rights to search for truth, to freely express and communicate one's opinions, and to be truthfully informed about public events; freedom of religion, democratic assembly, association and participation in political life; freedom to choose one's state in life; and to have these rights equally protected under the law. But the encyclical also goes beyond classical liberalism in incorporating socioeconomic rights developed under socialist welfare states. These rights include the right to life and the means necessary for the proper development of life: food, clothing, shelter, rest, medical care and social services, security in case of sickness, widowhood, old age, inability to work, unemployment or any other case where a person is unable to provide for him(her)self.[18]

The encyclical includes the rights to work, to choose one's work without coercion, to have safe working conditions and just wages and to organize associations and societies to promote these rights. The rights of working classes and of women to justice and to equal participation in public life are singled out for particular mention. Working classes are said to have gained ground in public affairs and can no longer be "treated as if they were irrational objects without freedom, to be used at the arbitrary disposal of others." (40) Women also are said to be now taking part in public life:

> Since women are becoming ever more conscious of their
> human dignity, they will not tolerate being treated as
> mere material instruments, but demand rights befitting
> a human person in both domestic and in public life. (41)

Seven months after the appearance of *Pacem in Terris,* the first draft of the Declaration on Religious Freedom was presented to the Second Vatican Council. In December 1965, the final version of this declaration was accepted by the Council. The declaration was controversial since it implied a repudiation of the teachings of the *Syllabus of Errors.* The declaration invokes the concept of "development of doctrine" to explain the disparity between the two, thereby avoiding an open admission that the previous teaching had been in error.

John Courtney Murray, the primary architect of the declaration, explains in an introduction to it that it contains three aspects: religious freedom as a human right, both personal and collective, the limitation of government in relation to the establishment of religion and the freedom of the Church vis-à-vis the sociopolitical order. These freedoms are not mere accommodation to necessity, but are integral to the Christian understanding to human dignity.

Murray also notes that the declaration leaves unaddressed the topic of the freedom of Christians within and in relation to the church itself.[19] Freedom of conscience within the church is the corollary of freedom of religion in society, and thus must be addressed in order to complete this "development of doctrine."

In the two decades since the Second Vatican Council, Catholic bishops in various countries have emerged as defenders of human rights, promoters of democratic freedom and economic justice in their societies. The bishops of Canada have issued a major statement on justice in the economic order, and the bishops of the United States of America have adopted a like document. The Canadian statement goes toward a democratic socialist society. The bishops defend the priority of the rights of all members of the society to full employment and a just wage against a system of maximization of profits that accepts a large percentage of unemployed people. The needs of the workers to have dignified work, adequate wages and basic social services takes priority, ethically, over government policies aimed at cutting inflation and maintaining high profit margins.

They also note that civil liberties in society are being eroded by government repression aimed at stifling protest against an unjust social order. The church must be a defender of human rights in this situation of growing repression.[20]

In Latin America repressive military regimes have arisen as the guardians of unjust economic systems, so this issue of defense of human rights is a more acute and immediate reality. In the national security states of contemporary neo-fascism,[21] a consistent human rights position becomes a radical and heroic option and puts nuns, priests and even bishops in danger of arrest, torture and assassination. In several Latin American countries, such as Chile and Brazil, the church has emerged as the one autonomous institution that can stand against right-wing dictatorships in defense of human rights. In established Communist states, such as Poland, the church also stands as the major autonomous institution that defends certain rights of dissent, religious and intellectual freedom and voluntary associations. The ambiguous defense of the free labor union, Solidarity, put some church leaders in lethal conflict with the Communist state.

Thus, in the last quarter of the twentieth century, it becomes possible to imagine that the Catholic Church might emerge from its cocoon in the European *ancien regime* to become a major defender of democratic and socialist values of political freedom and economic justice at a time when these values have been largely deserted by both communist and capitalist leaders. The Catholic Church is perhaps the major world institution that crosses the first, second and third worlds. The global church links together Catholic populations in Europe and North America, Eastern Europe and Latin America, Asia and Africa. The Pope is perhaps the only world leader that could get an enthusiastic reception in all three of these regions. If the Pope and bishops could speak credibly, out of a deep conviction of the best in the democratic and the socialist traditions, this would provide an invaluable witness in a world bereft of credible moral leadership in the social and political realm.

This opportunity of the church comes at a time when these values of political freedom and economic justice have become increasingly uncertain in secular society. Marxism was traditionally critical of liberalism because it saw questions of political equality as meaningless in an economic system of vast inequality of wealth. It assumed that human rights would automatically flourish once private ownership of the means of production was abolished for social ownership. But social ownership was interpreted to mean state ownership. Corporative, military societies, not unlike the fascist ideal, arose in the name of socialism, with special privileges for the managerial elites of the state bureaucracy. The critique of the limits of liberalism becomes an ideology for depriving the people of the political and cultural tools of dissent and change.

In the capitalist, industrial West the heritage of civil liberties is retained officially, but with great inequality in their actual exercise. These Western nations, particularly the United States, live in an exploitative relationship with Third World areas. Their affluence depends on the control of the cheap labor and raw materials of these dependent nations. Democratic values, such as free elections and a free press, are converted into ideological slogans for the defense of United States' political and economic control of these regions. "Defense of democracy" is used as a cover to win the acceptance of the American people for imperialist interventions in Nicaragua and other areas that are asserting their autonomy.

The United States and other nations of the "free world" have supported fascist regimes in Greece, Portugal, Spain, Central and South America and Southeast Asia, when such repressive military regimes were the cooperative tools of Western control. The United States, Britain and West Germany are unwilling to cut their ties to South Africa, despite the increasing violence and repression of basic civil liberties by which its government defends its racist system. Thus, in many places, the word "democracy" loses any real meaning since it has become a facade to cover brutal tyranny and economic exploitation. The farcical "free elections" in El Salvador, so acclaimed by the Reagan administration, is one example of this manipulation of democratic forms, without real substance, in order to maintain American hegemony.

However, it is not at all clear whether the Catholic Church, together with other Christian churches, can emerge as the defenders of a genuine democratic-socialist "center," against totalitarianisms of "left" and "right." This "middle way" too readily becomes a facade for the status quo, rather than a real alternative. The primary contradiction that prevents Roman Catholicism from standing as a real defender of democratic and socialist values is its inability to apply these values to itself as an institution. It is hard to take an institution seriously when it defends religious liberty, freedom of dissent, the equality of persons before the law, just wages and fair political processes, when it refuses to apply these principles within its own institutional walls.

The ethical double standard of human rights for secular societies, but monarchical absolutism for the church, means that church leaders have not really internalized these values and made them their own. They have not yet accepted the teachings of *Pacem in Terris* and the *Declaration on Religious Liberty* that human freedom and dignity is an integral part of the Christian gospel of creation and redemption. The second half of the "development of doctrine," the application of the doctrine of religious freedom to the church itself, envisioned by John Courtney Murray in 1965, has not yet taken place.

Indeed, under the papacy of John Paul II there has been a distinct regression, back to earlier practices of inquisitorial repression of free inquiry in the biblical, theological and ethical fields. The investigations of Edward Schillebeeckx, Leonardo Boff and Charles Curran, the depriving of Hans Küng of his *missio canonica* at the University of Tübingen and the harrassment of many lesser known figures, indicate that the spirit of the inquisition has returned to the Vatican.[22] It continues to be lodged in the renamed, but unchanged, Office of the Holy Inquisition, under Cardinal Ratzinger. Recent efforts of the Vatican to reassert direct control of seminaries, Catholic colleges and religious orders indicates that the principle of subsidiarity (local control) is hardly respected in practice and that the Roman model of government continues to be that of absolute monarchy.

The Catholic Church has adapted to liberal societies by developing a dualistic conception of church and state. The church is seen as a separate, divinely-founded institution, whose monarchical government is part of its essential nature as given by Christ. This hierarchical structure of the church is seen as immutable, continuing side by side with changeable secular political systems. Such a dualistic conception suggests that the church is indifferent to the political systems of secular society. It can work with imperial, feudal, monarchical, democratic, fascist or communist states, so long as it can gain its own freedom and autonomy as a church institution to do its own "purely religious" work. The church's primary business is the salvation of souls, not the reconstruction of the social order. The church must have the freedom to teach, to give the sacraments and to administer its own life. It influences society indirectly through the laity, but it does not intervene directly in secular matters, nor are secular governments to intervene in its life.

This dualistic concept of church and state of Catholic neo-liberalism stands behind recent admonitions of the Vatican and the American bishops against priests and nuns in political life. These admonitions echo the provisions of the Concordats with Hitler and Mussolini that forbade priests to be members of or active on behalf of political parties. These restrictions on priests and nuns in political life are mystifying, since they suggest that the church is, by nature, apolitical. Theologically speaking, such a dualism splits redemption from creation. Religion and politics are viewed as two separate realities, with no integral foundation. Politics belongs to purely "natural" life, unconnected with the church's mission of redemption.

Such a split of religion and politics has hardly been the general Catholic tradition or practice. Prior to modern liberal revolutions, the church was an integral part of Christian political states. Bishops were rulers of their territories, temporally as well as spiritually. The Pope himself fought a long battle to retain his claims to be the head of a temporal state, as well as the leader of the church, and still retains that status in diminished form. In the European *ancien regime*, bishops and priests were regarded as one of the three "estates" of society and took their places in European parliaments accordingly. Thus to maintain an absolute dividing line between church leaders and political activity as Catholic tradition is highly misleading.

What we actually have in this regulation against priests and nuns in political office is a modern adaptation to secular and sometimes anticlerical governments. In this situation the church seeks to retain complete control over its own ecclesiastical personnel, priests and religious. Their activities are to be limited to institutional structures directly controlled by the church itself. This means that the "church" consists primarily of this ecclesiastical personnel. The laity are not the church, but are persons who are to be taught and influenced by the church. Under the influence of the church's teaching, it is the laity who are the proper agents of secular, political activity.

The church itself, as an organization, operates as an autonomous institution over against "lay" society. As such, it is obviously a political institution. It engages in all sorts of political activity, direct and indirect, in relation to secular society, although this is concealed by labeling everything the church does as an institution as "religious" or "spiritual." Thus, what is really forbidden is not the church's involvement in politics, but rather the right of ecclesiastical personnel, nuns and priests to exercise political roles autonomous of the church as an institution, as office holders in state organizations not under church control.[23]

This dual theory of sacred church and secular governments allows the Catholic Church to exempt itself from the critique of human rights applied to society, and to fail to recognize itself as a historical institution. The claim that the church is essentially monarchical is questionable, both historically and theologically. Historically, it is evident that the church evolved from a congregational to a hierarchical and then to a monarchical structure by growing up within and imitating the imperial bureaucracy of the Roman Empire. It developed its hierarchical polity further by taking on feudal and then monarchical forms in medieval and early modern Europe. The political system of the Catholic Church is a historical construct, shaped by the political systems around it, not a divine given which has remained historically immutable.

Theologically, one must ask whether a democratic polity would not be a more appropriate expression of the community of salvation, than one modeled after Roman imperialism, medieval feudalism and Renaissance absolutism. The gospels give no evidence that Jesus left a clear directive on church polity. This is the more unlikely since early Christianity was shaped by an eschatological perspective and expected the imminent end of the world, not a long survival as a historical institution. But Jesus' teachings move in a very different direction from hierarchical and monarchical government. In Matthew 21:24-26 Jesus rebukes the power lust of his disciples by saying, "You know the rulers of the gentiles lord it over them (their subjects), and their great men exercise authority over them. It shall not be so among you, but whoever would be great among you must be your servant." A community of equals, rooted in the principle of mutual service, is the vision of the church in the gospels. Although church polities will ever reflect the changing political and social constructs around them, they should strive to find forms that best reflect this theological and ethical vision.

In the 1980's an American group, calling itself the Association for the Rights of Catholics in the Church, arose, declaring its purpose to be the writing of a charter of Rights of Catholics in the Church.[24] This group seeks to develop a consistent teaching on human rights, in which the rights affirmed by the church for society are applied to the church as well. This charter plants itself upon the dual foundations of "natural rights" and the rights of Christians as baptized members of the church. Among the rights it would win for all Catholics, lay as well as clerical, are the rights to have an informed conscience, freedom of speech, press and association in the church, access to information within the church, and teaching by church representatives based on wide consultation.

The charter also claims the right of all Catholics to have a voice in the decisions that affect them, to have their leaders accountable to the people and to express their dissent publicly in regard to decisions made by church authorities. Due process within the Catholic Church is also claimed. Accusations should be dealt with by just and impartial administrative and judicial procedures, and there should be regular channels for the redress of grievances. Theologians should have their academic freedom guaranteed at Catholic institutions. The charter goes on to claim other rights, such as the right to divorce and remarriage, to the ordination of women, and to choice of states of life, celibate or married, for the clergy. Reproductive rights and inclusive language are also seen as rights, under a charter of full human dignity for all members of the Catholic Church.

This charter is an important step toward a discussion of freedom in the Catholic Church. It needs to be developed in two ways. First, it should be evident that such human rights entail a structural reorganization of the Catholic Church. Basic assumptions such as the sovereignty of the people as the foundation of church polity, need to be elaborated. The church needs to be seen as arising from the people as a community, who then elect their own representatives on the local, regional, national and global levels, and hold these leaders accountable to the people.

Basic assumptions about the nature of truth need also to be developed. Traditional Vatican leadership has thought of truth as single, unitary and verbally definable. It has also believed that it has a special charism to define such truth in a way that makes it immune from ordinary human processes of verification through experience. The modern claim to freedom of thought and communication is based on the assumption that truth is partial and relative. Our knowledge and our ability to define reality is always approximate, at best. Truth is best served by a free marketplace of ideas. A community of scholarship arises that develops a working consensus about what is the best approximation of truth on any subject at a particular time. But it must remain open to the dissenting voice who may be the bearer of improved knowledge. This concept of freedom of thought finds its limits only in excluding those theories which would deny this freedom to inquiry to others in society.

If the Catholic Church is to adapt itself to this liberal understanding of truth, it must fundamentally rethink its traditional model of reason and revelation. Dogmatic pronouncements based on infallibility would become unacceptable.[25] This by no means rules out the capacity of the church to issue binding teaching. But this would be seen as a more modest claim to an informed consensus, offered to the free conscience of Christians, not something to be imposed coercively. It is interesting that in the recent pastoral letters of the Catholic bishops on nuclear war and on the economy, this more modest form of teaching authority has been adopted. The authority of these pronouncements has not suffered from this, but they have earned wider respect than recent pronouncements against birth control and women's ordination, handed down in the infallibilist style.

Finally, and most importantly, this development of freedom of conscience, human rights and democratic government in the church must be placed on a unified theological foundation, rather than on a dualistic separation of creation and redemption. What promotes the dignity of the human person in community "naturally" must also be seen as what the church is restoring and promoting in its redemptive mission. If the Catholic Church is to be a credible sign of salvation to the world, it must witness in its own institutional life to those values of freedom and human dignity that it now claims to promote in the world.

CHAPTER 2
SEXUAL QUESTIONS AND THE
CHALLENGE OF WOMEN

The second major challenge to the Catholic Church today has to do with sexual morality and the status of women. Fear of sexuality and the marginalization of women from church leadership are both deeply embedded in Catholic spirituality and polity. Both have a long history that goes back to early Christianity. The Jewish tradition from which Christianity arose, and the rabbinic legislation developing alongside early Christianity, had a more positive view of sexuality, although this was in the context of a patriarchal family and community. Not only were all Jews commanded to marry and procreate, but sexual intercourse itself was mandated on a regular basis to satisfy the sexual need of both partners. Jewish mysticism even saw in sexual union, particularly on the Sabbath, an expression of the reunification of the transcendent and immanent (male and female) sides of God.[1]

Jesus himself was not an ascetic, and there is no reason to believe that he mandated a celibate life style for his followers.[2] He seems to have been particularly forgiving toward women victimized by sexual exploitation, such as prostitutes or "women taken in adultery." The gospel tradition often contrasts the openness to faith of such women with the legalism and hostility to faith of the clerical elites.

However, in the first decades of the Christian mission Christianity was quickly caught up in the ascetic tendencies that were typical of radical religious movements in the Greco-Roman world. St. Paul linked celibacy with the coming eschatological age, which he believed would arrive very soon. He saw this as the preferable life style, but he did not forbid marriage.[3] In the first two centuries ascetic Christians, who saw conversion to chastity as the authentic Christian life style, battled with more conservative Christians who sought to maintain the Jewish traditions of patriarchal marriage and childbearing as normative for the Christian church, for clergy as well as laity.

In the late first and early second centuries Christians of both persuasions sought to claim Paul as their champion. In the Pastoral Epistles, written in Paul's name, a married clergy and patriarchally-ordered household, with subservient wife, children and slaves, are mandated for the Christian community. The Pauline doctrine of Original Sin is linked together with the Genesis stories of the secondary creation of woman and her primary responsibility for sin. This Christian *midrash* on Genesis (found nowhere else in Scripture) is employed to reject women's ministry in the church and to mandate childbearing as women's primary task. Through bearing children women will be forgiven their primacy in sin.[4]

This patriarchal and misogynist Pauline tradition contrasts sharply with an alternative Pauline tradition found in the *Acts of Paul and Thecla*. Here Paul calls a woman to chastity as the fullness of Christian conversion, in rejection of her previous betrothal in marriage. Thecla leaves home, dressed as a man, is pursued throughout the empire by the combined forces of state and family, and is vindicated by divine miracles. Her choice is blessed by Paul, at the culmination of the story, who commissions her to return to preach the gospel in her home town.[5]

In these conflicting Pauline traditions of early Christianity, defense of marriage and procreation was linked with the defense of the patriarchal family and social order. By contrast, ascetic rejection of marriage for chastity was connected to an egalitarian vision, in which the differences of sexual and social roles of men and women are dissolved in the spiritual equivalence of the redemptive order of Christ. Differences of Jew and Greek, slave and free, male and female are overcome in a new kind of redemptive community which allows all to preach and prophesy, according to the gifts of the Spirit. At first, the patriarchal, pro-marriage tradition won out in official Christianity against the ascetics, who would make celibacy normative for all Christians. The Pastoral Epistles were canonized, but the *Acts of Paul and Thecla*, while never condemned, were carried along as popular tradition.

However, by the fourth century the patriarchal and ascetic traditions begin to merge in a new way. Asceticism begins to become clericalized. The Council of Elvira in 400 A.D. mandated that all ordained priests and bishops withdraw from sexual congress with their wives.[6] Although the Christian clergy were still generally married, they were to be encouraged to live in brother-sister relations with their wives. A new monastic leadership arose in men like Jerome, Augustine and Basil the Great, who institutionalized asceticism in monastic communities separate from ordinary Christian communities. The ascetic life style is seen as higher than the married state. Monk-bishops created the ideal of a celibate clergy living in monastic community, although it would not be until the eleventh century in the Latin church that this was legally mandated for all priests. The Eastern church would continue to accept married priests, while bishops would be drawn from the monastic orders.

Patriarchal Christianity, since the late first century, had combated the egalitarian Christian inclusion of women in preaching and teaching. Ordained ministry was to be confined to men, although a female diaconate seems to have lingered on for several centuries. Female ascetics were segregated in cloisters as much as possible, under the supervision of bishops or their representatives. However, the autonomy of female communities continued to be reasserted throughout the centuries of Catholic Christianity. The modern conflict of popes and bishops with nuns is a recent chapter of a continuing saga.

Most of all, the synthesis of patriarchal and ascetic Christianity meant that asceticism was read primarily from the male and clerical point of view. Instead of asceticism being seen as releasing women from sexual and social subordination, women were viewed as dangerous threats to male sexual "purity".

The Christian clergy came to define itself primarily as a ritual priesthood, rather than as prophets or as teachers in the tradition of the rabbinate. Celibacy was linked with the sacral holiness of the priesthood, over against sexuality as the realm of sin and ritual pollution. In the sixth to ninth centuries the pollution taboos of Hebrew Scriptures were revived, defining all women, even nuns, by reason of their bodily functions, as ritually impure. Women were not to enter the sanctuary and were to touch sacred vessels only with covered hands. This union of asceticism with sacral priesthood decisively marginalized women from ministry and repressed those remnants of women's ministries in orders of deacons, widows and virgins in local churches.[7]

Women henceforth were either to be married and under the authority of their husbands, or confined to cloister and under the authority of bishops. The reality of women as nuns and as laywomen continued to defy these prescriptive limits. The clerical tradition of the medieval world would become characterized by increasingly vitriolic hostility to women. The outbreak of witch persecution in the late medieval and Reformation periods climaxed this clerical hostility to women as the demonic "other," especially when they were sexual, post-menopausal and outside male authority.[8]

The imposition of celibacy on all clergy, even in lower orders, in the eleventh century, was intended to remove churchmen from the feudal system, preventing church property from being inherited by children of priests. But for many village priests, it simply meant that their wives were demoted to concubines and their children defined as bastards. Married priests bitterly resented this imposition of celibacy by the monastic clergy, whom they suspected of being homosexuals and hence indifferent to the sexual needs of heterosexuals.[9] Abuses of the celibate system continued in the later Middle Ages. Monks and those in clerical orders in universities were seen as using their office to seduce women without taking responsibility for the resultant children. Bishops grew rich by exacting fines for illegitimate children from priests who lived with their common-law wives. These abuses generated increasing hostility which broke out in open protest in the Protestant Reformation.

In 1523, Martin Bucer, a German Dominican priest, publicly married, declaring that, while celibacy might be a gift given to a few, those who did not have it should marry rather than sin. In the fall of 1523 seven priests of the city of Strasbourg followed Bucer's example. They, too, declared that, while celibacy is a divine gift for some, most people are commanded by the rule of nature to marry. Moreover, they noted that it was the original custom of the church to have married clergy. A celibate priesthood was a recent, papal innovation.

Some of these priests were consecrating earlier, common-law relationships. By openly marrying they protested the laws of the church which defined such relationships as concubinage and their children as bastards. They were also expressing the increasing anger of ordinary townspeople against a celibate system that was expressed in rowdy young clerics who seduced their daughters and took no responsibility for their children. One of these new clergy brides, Catherine Zell, herself a Scripture scholar, preached a sermon in March of 1524 in which she accused the bishop of enforcing celibacy in order to collect taxes on concubines and to prevent clergy children from inheriting property. She defended the greater morality of marriage and denounced their irresponsible treatment of women and their children by priests.[10]

The marriages of these priests took place in the city cathedral before a large, applauding audience. The priests were excommunicated by the bishop but defended by the town council, who continued to give them access to the churches of the city. For a while the priest appointed by the bishop preached from the main pulpit of the cathedral, while the reformers preached from a makeshift pulpit rolled in on wheels. Then the city council voted to give sole support to the reformers, and the churches of Strasbourg became Protestant.

This scene in Strasbourg returns us to the atmosphere of anger against celibacy that brought about its rejection by the Reformation. One can well ask whether Catholics in the last decades of the twentieth century might be brought to a similar open defiance of clerical celibacy. The difference between the sixteenth century and today, however, is that there are no princes or town councils who can hand the churches over to the reformers. That integration of church and magistrates was brought to an end by the liberal revolutions of the nineteenth century. The struggle for reform must be waged today within a church institution where clerical power is unchecked by lay power.

The Reformation not only rejected celibacy for the clergy, it also swept away monastic life as well. It affirmed the goodness of marriage as the normal state of life of Christians. Celibacy was no longer seen as a higher state of holiness for a religious or clerical elite. However, the Reformation assumed the patriarchal form of marriage. The household codes that mandated the subordination and obedience of wives to husbands, children to parents and servants to masters was stressed all the more as the proper order of marriage and society. The efforts of left-wing Protestants, such as Baptists and Quakers, to claim the preaching ministry for women, on the grounds of the equality of the sexes in Christ, was fiercely repressed by the mainline reformers.[11] Although Puritans particularly stressed the need for loving companionship between spouses, this was always within a framework of male dominance.[12]

Women also lost the autonomous education and leadership they had enjoyed, to some extent, in women's religious orders. The Catholic Church responded to the Reformation attacks by efforts to reform the abuses of celibate and monastic life. But, for women's religious orders, these reforms aimed largely at reenforcing strict cloister for women and the subordination of women's orders to male supervision, both within the community itself and in its relations to the outside world.[13] Thus, although the Reformation elevated the status of marriage and initiated the development of the modern idea of companionate married couples, overall the status of women was not enhanced by the Reformation. In some ways the Protestant and Catholic Reformations reenforced social trends that were further marginalizing women, economically and socially.[14]

It would be the liberal revolutions of the late eighteenth and nineteenth centuries that would set loose the modern demand for women's political equality. Feminism as a part of liberal reformism would seek the equal access of women to political decision-making, education and professional employment, including the ordained ministry. Modern medicine would curb the death rate which had previously killed two-thirds of the children before adulthood. The shift from farming to industrial ecomony meant that the large family was no longer economically viable. All this brought the demand for medically safe and effective methods of birth control out into the open. The sexual revolution would challenge the traditional Christian ethics of sex as sinful outside of procreative marriage. The modern stress on companionate marriage would also suggest that marriages that have grown hostile should be dissolved and the partners should be allowed to try again. Catholicism, which had resisted all these reforms and changes of viewpoint from the Reformation to the 1950's, was thus cast in the position, after the Second Vatican Council, of having to deal with all of them simultaneously.

Issues related to sexual ethics and to the status of women have become the primary areas of controversy in the postconciliar Catholic Church. Clerical celibacy, hierarchical control over women religious, divorce, reproductive rights, homosexuality and the ordination of women are all flash points of ideological controversy. All these issues intertwine around basic attitudes toward sexuality and toward control over women forged by the Catholic Christian synthesis of patriarchal and ascetic religious ideology. All these issues represent not only areas of theoretical conflict over ethics, but areas of control of a male celibate hierarchy over an ecclesiastical institution based on male over female, celibate over sexual. The traditional view in each case is typically asserted as unchangeable teaching despite the poorly developed theoretical basis of that teaching, and the fact that it is under question by moral theologians, as well as by large sections of the Catholic people most directly affected. Thus every argument over sexual morality and women becomes a conflict over authority and obedience to authority.

As we have seen in this chapter, celibacy began in Christianity as a lay tradition of holiness, not as a requirement for ordination. Its imposition on the ordained clergy was slow and imperfect in the Middle Ages. The Catholic Counter Reformation sought to tighten these controls over priests and also over nuns and monks and to prevent further abuses. While this has perhaps been more successful in Germanic and Irish culture than in Latin culture, the effect has been more of hiding lapses from sight, rather than preventing them altogether. Since celibacy, in the legal sense of the unmarried state, is seen as a requirement for office or religious status, this results in a policy which is more lenient toward the clerics who "fall" into illicit sex, but without moral commitment, than toward the men who wish to build committed relationships sanctified by marriage.

Sexual peccadillos are seen as endlessly forgiveable as long as the priest repudiates his sexual partner and repents. But the priest who wishes to marry is treated as a pariah. He is expected to vanish from sight, his name never to be mentioned again in the Catholic community. All the skills and knowledge that he has built up through his training and service are treated as worthless. It is better for him to disappear rather than cause "scandal." Nuns and monks who departed from their religious communities to marry, or simply to return to lay life, were also treated with similar inhumanity.

Recently there have been efforts to reform the sheer brutality and waste of talent involved in this treatment of laicized priests and ex-nuns. Some religious orders have developed a severance allowance to help the ex-nun to build a new life. Some orders have even expanded their definition of religious life to include tertiary membership for such persons. Colleges have sought to retain faculty members in employment when they change their status from priest to layman. But the Vatican, particularly under John Paul II, has shown no disposition to support this more lenient treatment of those who depart from their vows.[15]

This crisis over celibacy takes place in a contemporary culture that finds little credibility in the dualistic anthropology that traditionally supported asceticism. Sexuality is no longer seen as a lower part of the self that must be repressed in order to strength one's higher moral and intellectual faculties. Rather, sexuality is seen as an integral part of one's total psychosomatic energy and capacity for relationship. Modern psychology throws doubt upon whether anyone can be psychologically mature if one has not integrated one's sexuality into one's overall personhood. Many who want to be priests thus come to wonder whether celibacy is psychologically healthy. Although the rhetoric of celibacy as a "gift" may still be used, it is no longer clear what sort of a "gift" this really is. If this simply means a lack of emotional affect, this hardly seems to make for wholesome persons.

Traditional celibate socialization focused on avoidance of contact with women, particularly intimate contact that might lead to affection. But since priests will have to pastor women in their congregations, such avoidance scarcely lent itself to either good pastoral care of women or emotional maturity of priests. Some seminaries have tried to correct this by bringing their seminarians into contact with women as students in other theological degree programs or in conjunction with Protestant seminaries where women can be ordained. Women have been hired as pastoral counselors and teachers of pastoral counseling. But this has drawn the wrath of the Vatican whose efforts to regain control over Catholic seminaries takes the form of forbidding women as pastoral counselors and discouraging the presence of women students.[16] Thus two fundamentally different understandings of moral development are in conflict in this controversy.

Homosexuality is a second issue that divides not only Catholics, but Protestants as well. Most Christian churches remain committed officially to the traditional view that only heterosexual sexuality within marriage is licit. Homosexuality is a violation of "nature" and is always sinful. Some Christian church leaders may acknowledge the modern psychological view that homosexual orientation may be a fixed part of some people's nature, but this is seen as a handicap or failure of development. Although such people may be acknowledge to "be" homosexual, i.e., attracted sexually to people of their own gender and not to people of the other gender, they are not to "act" upon this attraction. Thus celibacy is recommended for all homosexuals, whether or not they are ordained.[17]

Needless to say, few homosexuals find this recommendation of lifetime celibacy an adequate response to their sexual feelings and needs. Gay Christian support groups have sprung up in most Christian denominations to provide religious nurture and community for Christian homosexuals. Dignity functions as such a group for Catholic homosexuals, and New Ways Ministries focuses particularly on pastoral care for gay priests and lesbian nuns. These groups have been given negative treatment by bishops since it is obvious that they do not function within the official ethical guidelines on homosexuality but are advocacy groups for an alternative sexual ethic.[18]

In 1977 the Catholic Theological Society of America published a major study of human sexuality that explored such an alternative ethic. The CTSA report suggested that Catholic moral theology should move from a legalistic to a relational sexual ethic. The core of moral sexuality is moral relationality, according to the report. Healthy relationality is not achieved all at once but is a question of moral development. The goal is to move toward relationships which are faithful, loving, mutual and life-enhancing, and away from relationships which are violent, unfaithful, deceitful, manipulative and exploitative. The report suggests that homosexuality should be seen as a variant of sexual orientation that occurs naturally, like left-handedness, in ten to twelve percent of the population. Homosexuals, like heterosexuals, should be encouraged to develop committed relationships which are faithful, loving and mutual.

This new criterion of sexual morality threatened to obliterate the neat boundaries between sinful homosexual, unmarried or non-procreative sex, and moral heterosexual, married and procreative sex. Much married heterosexual, procreative sex might be immoral because it is violent, exploitative and lacking in mutual enhancement of the personal development of both partners. But a committed homosexual relationship, or a more temporary and unmarried but faithful and loving relationship, might be seen as having positive moral value. The report was not accepted by the American Catholic biships, but it continues to stand as a challenge and alternative to the traditional Catholic sexual ethics.

The question of homosexuality challenges Catholic institutionalized sexual sociology on two fronts. On the one hand, it challenges the traditional restriction of moral sexuality to procreative heterosexual marriage. It suggests that sexuality can be separated from procreational functionality and find an autonomous meaning and ethic as an expression of love and relationship. Secondly, it exposes the ambiguity of celibate priesthood and religious orders. New Ways Ministries estimates from their experience that about half of American Roman Catholic priests consider themselves homosexual. There is no way to know if this represents a recent increase or not. One might guess that the contemporary emphasis on sexuality as an integral part of one's personality has caused more priests to claim their sexual orientation consciously. Perhaps fewer heterosexuals are willing to take vows of celibacy, while homosexuals see celibacy as a shield.

The last ten years also saw a quiet breakdown in the social disciplines that kept priests in seminaries and in the parish in a celibate life style. It has become common for priests to have a "second life," apart from their clerical life, where they pursue homosexual or heterosexual experience, whether this means the underworld of bars or a separate household where they live with a lover. There have also been a series of scandals involving priests in sexual abuse of boys in the parish.[19] Bishops have shown a notable tendency to cover up these incidents, and to look the other way at this underworld of sexual activity, so long as it doesn't involve committed married relationships. Needless to say, this kind of double life does not make for good moral development in the Catholic clergy or good pastoral care for parishioners. The removal of most of the governing authority of his diocese from Archbishop Hunthausen of Seattle, Washington, a beloved pastor known for his outspoken opposition to nuclear war, seems to have occurred, in large part, because of his pastoral approach to questions of homosexuality among the priests of his diocese.

Catholic laity are becoming increasingly aware that they are not well served by the present system of clerical celibacy. Celibacy is one of the major causes of a decline in adequate numbers of ordained priests, at a time when Protestants are experiencing an oversupply of clergy. Bishops are reluctant to weed out unfit men who are ordained. Women and married men who would like to minister are prevented from doing so as a part of the ordained ministry. Thus a male celibate clergy is being maintained at the expense of the needs of the people for an adequate pastoral ministry. One effort to extend the ministry has been the acceptance of a married male diaconate, but these men are clearly second-class citizens in the clergy. Moreover, elements of the ascetic ethic are imposed on them by forbidding them to remarry, if they are widowed, or to marry if they are single at the time of ordination.[20]

The continuing rejection of a married (male) priesthood involves some elements of power and money. A married priesthood would require the maintenance of a wife and family. It would also be less at the disposal of hierarchical authority, less able to be moved around at will. It would not belong to the same extent to a separate clerical culture. But the chief reason is the continuing link between sacramental purity and celibacy. Sexuality is seen as polluting the purity and holiness of the priest and his sacramental status. It is assumed by bishops that the laity believe and want this, but, in fact, a married priesthood would be readily accepted by the laity. This mentality belongs essentially to a clerial culture that believes itself superior, by virtue of its celibacy, to married people.

One married priest, Frank Bonnike, wrote in the May-June 1986 issue of *Corpus Reports*, a newsletter for an organization of married priests, about his experiences as a hospital chaplain. For him, marriage and fatherhood has greatly improved his ability to minister because he understands the lives of lay people much better. He has become much more sensitive to the vicissitudes of family life. People are willing to confide in him much more than they did when he was a celibate. He also feels that his marriage has made him more sensitive to women's experiences. He writes:

> The celibacy question in the Church is really a woman's issue. The institutional Church is somehow saying that my wife, other priests' wives and Eve, have corrupted priests who have married and somehow left them ministerially impotent . I assure you the opposite is true. Women have so much to teach us men about the persons to whom we minister.[21]

Underlying this hostility to women either as priests' wives or as priests themselves, lies an obsolete anthropology which regarded women as lacking full human nature and being in a state of subjugation due to their presumed greater guilt for sin. This argument, developed by Thomas Aquinas, borrowing the biology and patriarchal sociology of Aristotle, originally did not simply exclude women from ordination, but was a general argument against women's public leadership and autonomy in society in general. The opposition of the Pope and the American bishops to women's suffrage in the early decades of the twentieth century reflected this view that women should remain confined to the domestic role and must be under male authority.[22]

In the 1975 Vatican Declaration Against Women's Ordination, there is an effort to abandon this historic connection between a patriarchal social order and the denial of ordination to women. Using recent feminist scholarship, the Declaration says that the gospel promotes equality between the sexes and implies that the church has always promoted women's equality in society. While there may be elements of truth in the first half of the statement, the second half is a flat denial of the actual historical tradition of the Catholic Church toward women. The Declaration tries to separate the question of women's social status from ordination. The exclusion of women from priesthood is related to a Christological mystery. It is said that there must be a physical resemblance between the priest and Christ. Needless to say, this physical resemblance is not extended to Semitic facial features. It is maleness that is regarded as the sacramental matter that makes the priest like Christ.[23]

Lurking behind such sacramentalizing of maleness lies the Thomistic-Aristotelian anthropology which believed that women were imperfect humans and hence could not represent perfect or normative human nature. In order for Christ to represent the fully human, he must be male. The maleness of God and the maleness of the image of God, the divine Word, is also suggested in this Christology. Thus the maleness of Christ, and his representative, the priest, is required in order to represent both God and perfect man.[24]

Such a masculinist theology threatens to exclude women, not only from ordination, but from redemption as well. If women can't represent Christ, then it becomes questionable if Christ represents women. Christ is incarnated only into maleness, not into a humanity that includes men and women. The church no longer represents a new humanity in Christ, in which there is neither male nor female, but all are one in Christ" (Gal 3:28). Thus the defense of patriarchal clericalism results in the final denial of the universal claims of the gospel.

Despite the efforts of the Declaration to separate ordination from social status, and to declare the church wholeheartedly on the side of women's equality in secular society, there is little evidence that the Vatican and the bishops have really changed their patriarchal view of the family and social order. In the 1970's the American bishops steadfastly refused to endorse the Equal Rights Amendment that would guarantee to women equality before the law. One of the major expressions of this hostility to women's autonomy lies in the opposition of the Catholic Church to birth control.

Historically, the condemnation of birth control was linked with an ascetic view of sexuality that saw sex as inherently the expression of the sinful impulse of concupiscence. Sexuality was allowed, or "forgiven" (made venially sinful), if it was used only for procreation within marriage and the unfortunate side effects of pleasure were scorned as much as possible. But, if sexual intercourse was separated from procreation, even within marriage, then it became pure lust or mere fornication, no better than the brothel. This was the sexual ethics bequeathed to Catholic Christianity by St. Augustine.[25]

Augustine would also allow a second purpose of sexuality as the "remedy of concupiscence." Needless to say, it was male concupiscence he had in mind. The male sexual impulse was seen as a tempestuous demand that would run amok and corrupt the other good wives of the society unless it was confined to one's own legitimate wife. Augustine also defended the necessity of prostitutes on the same ground, as better than the corruption of married women by men other than their husbands. Prostitutes are compared by Augustine to sewers. filthy but necessary for the good order of the city.[26] It is not far-fetched to see that, in such a view of sexuality, each man's wife is his private sewer into which he dumps his lust, so that it won't flow outside into the streets. What is left completely undeveloped in this view is any understanding of sexuality as love and expression of relationship.

In the 1960's Catholic moral theologians, and also married people, began to question this narrow view of the purposes of sexuality and the resulting rejection of artificial contraception. Some relaxation of the classical view had already taken place in the reluctant acceptance of the "safe period" method of birth control, i.e., spacing births by avoiding sexual intercourse during the time of the month when the woman is fertile. But the methods for predicting this time were uncertain, and married people jokingly referred to this type of birth control as "Vatican roulette." Once it had been accepted that sexuality had a legitimate purpose in the expression of love, while consciously avoiding conception, the effort to make an absolute moral distinction between mechanical barriers and elaborate temperature-taking and secretion-testing to ascertain one's fertile period seemed unconvincing. Moreover, the invention of the birth control pill in the 1960's made it possible to suppress ovulation altogether until it was desired for the creation of a child.

During the Vatican Council in the early 1960's, a number of books were written by moral theologians and theologically-educated lay people challenging the traditional teaching on contraception.[27] In response to this criticism Pope Paul VI convened a special birth control commission which met between 1964 and 1967. The commission was unusual since it showed an effort to consult a wide range of experts, not only theologians but sociologists and married couples. The personal testimony of married couples made a great impression on clerics, used to thinking about sexuality and reproduction in scholastic categories. A changed understanding of the meaning of sexuality and family planning in the context of marriage emerged from the meetings of the commission. This was the basis of the final majority report, which recommended the acceptance of artificial birth control as morally legitimate within committed, child-raising marriage.[28]

But a conservative minority found it impossible to reconcile this change with the authority of the earlier tradition. Patty Crowley, who, together with her husband, Pat Crowley, had represented the Catholic Family Movement on the commission, recalls a scene with a conservative cardinal in the last days of the work of the commission. The cardinal declared that he did not see how the church could change its previous teaching, asking what would happen to all those condemned to Hell because of their violation of the past prohibitions. Patty Crowley replied to him, "But, Your Eminence, do you really think that God has obeyed all your orders?"[29]

Pope Paul VI chose to disregard the conclusions of the final document of the Commission. In 1968 he reaffirmed the traditional ban on artificial birth control in his encyclical *Humanae Vitae*. The enclyclical evoked a storm of protest from lay people, and from some theologians and priests as well. Most lay people simply chose to disregard the encyclical and to continue to practice contraception. The conflict began to make clear that papal authority could no longer count on passive acquiescence to its teachings, if this failed to respect the informed consciences of the Catholic people. It also suggests that one of the major barriers to rethinking traditional teaching on sexuality, or any other subject, lay in the notion of irreformable authority. Hans Küng, leading German conciliar theologian, took this as the impetus to write a major book challenging the doctrine of infallibility.[30]

Although the teaching on contraception had lost its credibility with moral theologians and with the laity, it still continued to be maintained. It has even been reaffirmed, in relation to Third World nations with pressing population problems, by Pope John Paul II. This Pope had been a member of the papal birth control commission of 1964-7, but he never attended any of its meetings and so remained uninfluenced by the development of consciousness that seemed to have affected some other prelates on the commission.[31] In 1984 the Vatican investigation of Charles Curran, a moderately dissenting Catholic ethicist who had been under fire in the 1960's, was revived. Despite careful efforts to qualify his position, Father

Curran was declared by the Sacred Congregation as unfit to teach Catholic moral theology in August of 1986. Thus the Pope seems determined to turn back the clock and restore the consensus[32] against birth control that had disappeared in the late 1960's.

In the 1970's and 80's the battleground over reproductive rights moved from birth control to abortion The Catholic hierarchy joined with conservative Protestants in this crusade, who likewise saw opposition to abortion as the primary battleground against feminism The rhetoric of this debate has been highly misleading. The anti-abortion group seeks to take the high ground of defense of life, even though most of their leadership had little record of support of life-enhancing issues for humans after birth Some bishops sought to become more consistent by linking anti-abortion and anti-nuclear war in what was called a seamless garment of pro-life issues. But major anti-abortion leaders objected to this seamless garment approach, since they knew that their primary constituency lay with conservative groups that oppose gun control and support the arms race.[33]

Those who seek to defend legal abortion have not done a good job in persuading the American public either. By using the language of pro-choice, they have conveyed the impression that abortion itself is morally neutral or even desirable. Although some pro-choice people may think that abortion is morally neutral, no one thinks that abortion is a positive or desirable experience in itself. Even if no longer life-threatening under proper medical conditions, abortion remains an experience that ranges from sad to traumatic. It is not something any women would seek for its own sake. Rather, it is a desperate remedy for a previous evil; namely, the loss of reproductive self-determination. Any women who want an abortion (other than a small percentage who seek it because of a deformed fetus), are women who have already lost their reproductive self-determination. An unwanted pregnancy has been forced upon them against their will by a combination of ignorance, sexual coercion and inadequate medical means.

Pro-choice, essentially, is seeking to enhance women's reproductive self-determination, so that they will be able to choose, as fully as possible, when they wish to bear and raise a child and when they do not. The possibility of such a choice is fundamental to the establishment of a woman's full human dignity and capacity for self-determination in other areas of her life. As long as she is subject to unchosen childbearing, it is difficult or impossible for her to choose to develop her other capacities for public leadership and employment, in combination with chosen maternity and family life. Pro-choice thus means, finally, the positive experience of choosing to have a child at a particular time in one's life, by not having to live in fear of unchosen pregnancies.

The anti-abortion movement in the Catholic Church, as well as in other conservative sectors of society, basically oppose this option of reproductive self-determination for women. They want a woman's body to be at the disposal of her husband, nature and "God," who determine her destiny. Motherhood is seen as the primary meaning of women's identity. For them a woman's right to decide when she will bear a child deprives the whole patriarchal system of society, and its ruling God, of its fundamental power, the power over life, that is guaranteed by making women's bodies the adjunct of male acts of will and decision making. For women to become the decision makers over reproduction is to overthrow the material and ideological base of the entire hierarchy of male power over women, based on control over women's capacity to bear children.

That the essential issue in the abortion issue is control over women, and women's child-bearing capacity, becomes evident when we see that the anti-abortion movement not only does not support pro-life issues after birth, but also consistently oppose contraception and sex education for youth. Even in inner-city high schools, where poverty is running rampant and teenage pregnancy is a key part of this cycle of poverty, abortion foes clamor against the availability of contraceptive information for these teenagers. Clearly, if one was really interested in reducing the evils of abortion, the best way to do so would be to enhance all the aspects of culture that could help women to resist unwanted sexuality and to prevent unchosen pregnancy.

Reducing teen pregnancy is a complex issue, since many poor young women accept sexual relations with young men, who have no intention of taking responsibility for them or their children, and become pregnant as a way of getting out of abusive homes and into the meager autonomy of the welfare rolls. In order to turn around this pattern of teenage pregnancy, one has to examine all the factors in this train of events. Unquestionably, adequate information about and use of contraception is a fundamental factor in enhancing the self-determination of these women, although it must be combined with other aspects, such as the likelihood of jobs after education is completed. Thus, abortion foes who oppose birth control and sex education are actually promoting both the high abortion rates and the poverty cycle of teenage, unwed mothers that they claim to oppose.

In 1984-5 the efforts of the Catholic hierarchy to block women's reproductive self-determination, and hence women's general autonomy as agents of their own life plan, became dramatically intertwined with its efforts to reassert control over American religious women. Anti-abortion rhetoric had become a major political weapon by which conservatives attacked social progressives. The American hierarchy had become increasingly willing to breach the separation of church and state by telling Catholics that they could not support political candidates that accepted legal abortion. This dictate included Catholic candidates especially, even if they declared that they themselves did not favor abortion, but supported the right of others to choose it when it did not violate their conscience. This was the public position of Democratic vice-presidential nominee, Italian Catholic Geraldine Ferraro.

When Archbishop O'Connor of New York told Catholics they could not vote for a person with such a position, he was, in effect, trying to deprive the Democratic presidential ticket of the traditionally Democratic Catholic vote. Liberal Catholics sought to oppose this political intervention of the Catholic hierarchy by publishing an ad in the *New York Times* that declared that the official position on abortion was not morally definitive, and that Catholic moral theologians, with good conscience, could promote alternative views. One hundred Catholic leaders signed the ad, including twenty-three nuns.[34] The hierarchical response was swift. By March the nuns signing had received letters sent by the Vatican to their religious superiors declaring that they must recant their position or resign from their congregations. Lay signers also felt pressure, either efforts to remove them from positions in Catholic institutions or to prevent them from speaking in Catholic institutions on any subject. But the primary pressure point of the Vatican was on the nuns.

The nuns generally resisted making any open recantation of their position, but most ended with compromise statements that allowed them to remain in their religious communities. These religious women found this experience shocking and demoralizing. The religious women who signed the ad were the American leaders of feminist, social justice and anti-war movements among Catholic women. It was evident that the Vatican was willing to sacrifice the presence of this whole community of women in order to reassert its control over nuns and over the official teaching on reproductive rights. This struggle over the *New York Times* ad also coincided with a series of directives from the Vatican aimed at reasserting control over women's religious congregations. Renewed and democratized congregations were ordered to submit their constitutions to Rome. Those judged inadequately hierarchical were sent back for revision.

The Congregation of the Sisters of Mercy of the Union was particularly hard hit by these directives. Their president, Teresa Kane, had publicly requested that the Pope reconsider his position on women's ordination during his visit to the United States in 1979. The Sisters of Mercy of the Union seemed to be subjected to a vendetta from the Vatican after that event.[35] Strict surveillance of the policies on sterilization in their hospitals was one area of conflict. Another was the question of nuns in public political office. Three of their sisters were forced to resign from the community because they held political office. Only one of these incidents had any connection with reproductive rights, that of Sister Agnes Mary Mansour, who had accepted an appointed position as Director of Social Services for the state of Michigan. This department administered funds for abortion. Although Mary Mansour stated that she herself did not support abortion, as director she had to follow the current law and make such funds available to those entitled to them.

Two other nuns holding public office also were forced to resign from the community because of their unwillingness to give up elected public office. In both cases the grounds for this demand from the hierarchy was that nuns were forbidden to hold public office, a limitation that had not previously been directed at nuns until the papacy of John Paul II. It is significant that the Vatican Council had defined nuns as lay women. Yet, the hierarchy now clearly regarded nuns as the bottom layer of a system of clerical professionals who must remain within the control of the official institution, and not serve in political bodies outside such control.

All of these sex-related issues, male clerical celibacy, the opposition to the ordination of women or even their admission to minor ministerial roles such as altar servers, denial of reproductive rights and reassertion of control over nuns indicate that underneath these various issues lies a general inability of an ascetic patriarchal church to deal with women as autonomous moral agents and human persons of equal dignity and status with males. It is unlikely that there will be substantial progress on any of these issues without some kind of conversion of Catholic male celibate leadership to a more affirmative view of women's full humanity.

CHAPTER 3
THE CHALLENGE
OF THE THIRD WORLD

Historically, Roman Catholicism has been the Church of Western Europe. Its spread to the Americas, Africa and Asia was closely related to French, Portuguese and Spanish colonial expansion. To keep Portugal and Spain from competing with each other over the newly explored lands, Pope Alexander VI in 1493 drew a line on the map of the world running from pole to pole dividing the spheres of influence between these two Catholic colonial powers. The Catholic powers were given responsibility to convert the natives to the Catholic faith in the process of taking their lands and enslaving their bodies. Thus the Catholic faith arrived in these lands very much as the auxiliary to the sword.

Not all churchmen quietly acquiesced in the enslavement and slaughter of the native peoples of these continents. The Dominican friar and later the bishop of Chiapas, Bartolome de las Casas, repeatedly complained to the Spanish authorities about the brutal treatment of the Indians.[1] He was named by Cardinal Ximenes de Cisneros, who was acting as regent for the Spanish king, as Protector of the Indians. But de las Casas' efforts had little practical effect. The Spanish continued to regard the Indians as naturally inferior and to justify their enslavement or slaughter accordingly. The Aristotelian doctrine that the "barbarians" are natural slaves in relation to the Hellenes[2] (which was read to mean Christians), was readily applied to the dark-skinned natives of Africa and the Americas. Spanish Catholics also shared with Jews and Muslims the reading of the story of the sons of Noah that designated the Africans as the descendents of Ham who were condemned to be hewers of wood and drawers of water.[3]

Not only were the peoples of these continents presumed to be inferior to the Christian Europeans, but their culture and religious traditions were generally seen as worthless. Here again there was some resistance by more enlightened churchmen. The Jesuit missionaries to India and China particularly contended that these cultures had already received a preparation for the gospel through a general revelation available naturally to all humans. Chinese and Indian Christianity should build upon and be expressed in the context of the cultural traditions of these regions, much as it had built upon and been expressed in the Greco-Roman philosophical culture of the third and fourth centuries, for the peoples of the Hellenistic world of the late Roman Empire.[4]

But these enlightened views of cultural indigenization of Christianity were eventually suppressed in favor of a European ethnocentrism which regarded Catholic Christianity and European civilization as being of one piece. To be converted to Christianity was, at the same time, to have one's native culture wiped away, to be replaced by the superior culture of the Western European. This debate over cultural indigenization of Christianity is by no means over in 1986. In his recent trips to Africa, Pope John Paul II has been hostile to efforts to incorporate drumming and other native forms of worship into the Catholic Mass in that region.[5]

For most of the missionaries of the colonial era, conversion to Christianity meant, at the same time, docile acquiescence to their colonial masters. Hierarchical government and European rule were seen as divinely ordained. To submit to these masters was to submit to God. To rebel against them was to rebel against God. Christianity was a tool of pacification of colonized peoples. By accepting the gospel of Christ these conquered people were to internalize their own subjugation.

After more than three hundred years of Spanish and Portuguese colonial rule in Latin America, anticolonial rebellions broke out in these regions, inspired by the examples of the American and the French Revolutions in the late eighteenth century. Since the Catholic Church was seen as an integral part of the system of colonial rule, most of the revolutionaries of Latin America were militantly anticlerical. As in North America, where the revolution was led by the planter and merchant classes of the thirteen colonies, the Latin anticolonial revolutions were led by the creoles or native-born Spanish, who had no intention of liberating Indians and Blacks, but rather of taking power themselves. One of the more radical revolutionary figures was, however, a priest, Father Hidalgo, whose *grito* (cry) to revolution in 1810 caused mass uprisings among Indians who rallied to the banner of the Virgin of Guadalupe.

Hidalgo was not able to sustain the revolutionary fervor he had unleashed and was captured and shot a year and a half later. But the revolutionary banner was picked up by a more capable leader, José Maria Morelos, also a priest. He enunciated the ideals of an independent, republican, socially-egalitarian Mexico. Tribute and slavery would be abolished, and, although still Catholic in faith, the church would be stripped of its immense material possessions, particularly in land. He, too, was executed, but not before he had organized the revolutionary effort for five years. It would not be until 1822, in the wake of revolutionary turmoil in Spain itself, that the independence of Latin America (with the exception of a few areas, such as Cuba and Puerto Rico) would be complete.

The radical priest leaders of the Mexican revolution were exceptional, and were regarded by church leaders as heretics as well as rebels.[6] The clergy generally clung to royal absolutism and set its face against both independence and liberal principles. The first decades after independence were characterized by the rise of *caudillos* or dictators in the emergent nations. By mid-century new reformers were on the rise, inspired by liberal principles. Separation of church and state, religious toleration, democratization, and land reform (which included confiscation and selling of church lands) were part of the liberal agenda. Again the leadership of the Catholic Church bitterly opposed these reforms, siding with the conservative landed ruling classes. Pius IX condemned the reforming constitution of Mexico, shaped by new leaders such as Benito Juarez, and the Mexican hierarchy threatened anyone who upheld it with excommunication.

These struggles led to a full-scale civil war, with defense of church and property pitted against reform. The Laws of Reform, issued by Juarez, separated church and state, permitted toleration of all faiths, closed convents, ended tithings, required civil marriage and confiscated church property other than that used directly for worship. Throughout the nineteenth century and into the first decades of the twentieth century, the Catholic Church in Latin America, as in Europe, pitted itself against liberalism at every turn.

In the 1920's, in the aftermath of the third major Mexican revolutionary effort, there was open religious war between priests and their supporters and government forces inspired by militant secularism. Once again church land was confiscated, priests driven out of many states, and priests and nuns forbidden to wear clerical garb on the streets. Although the militant secularists were by no means always inspired by noble principles—many simply wanted church wealth for themselves and their followers—these actions were widely supported because the church was seen as anti-revolutionary, the bastion of traditional wealth and privilege.

The 1930-1960 period saw some shifts in this hostility between Catholicism and the liberal democratic ideals. The Catholic clergy began to adapt to the separation of church and state by supporting lay movements, such as Catholic Action, that were intended to permeate society with Christian principles. The priest was to act indirectly, as chaplain to these movements, rather than directly as a political leader. Christian democratic parties were created as expressions of the search for a "middle way" between right-wing military autocracy and communism, with its militant secularism. Industrial development, helped by investment by wealthy industrialized countries of Western Europe and the United States, was expected to overcome crushing poverty and stem the tide of more revolutionary movements.

In Mexico these Christian democratic and developmentalist ideals were expressed by the church-supported party PAN (Partido de Accion National). Its hopes were expressed in terms such as the following, taken from a party statement of 1960:

> . . .the Party of National Action (PAN) has proclaimed that the only genuine and effective way to curb the spread of communism in Mexico is to make a valiant and consistent effort to provide social justice based on integrity and honesty of purpose. The goals of PAN are to provide, among other points, a decent minimum wage for labor and rural workers; the participation of labor in the profits of the employer, as well as all the other benefits provided within a Christian democratic structure. Our party wishes to establish a sound and stable basis of operation for the worker and the investor in order to raise the standard of living of our people and to bring about a more equitable distribution of our national wealth.[7]

But the 1960's saw increasing challenges to these Christian democratic and developmentalist hopes. A new school of Latin American economists challenged the idea that Latin America was "underdeveloped" and merely needed First World investment in order to "take off" on a path of industrialization parallel to that of North America. Latin American economies, they said, were not underdeveloped, but misdeveloped. Their poverty is the underside of centuries of dependency during which their natural resources were stripped, through exploitative use of cheap or slave labor, to provide the wealth for the development of the colonizing nations. New investment and government aid would not change this distorted pattern of relationship, since it took place within the same system of dependency and exploitation. The profits from such investment, controlled from abroad, would be drained off into the pockets of the foreign investors and would not create an integral development that would provide the jobs and goods needed by Latin Americans as a whole.[8]

Moreover, these critical economists saw the situation worsening in the late 1960's. Formerly Latin American economies had been kept in dependency to provide cheap labor and agricultural and other raw materials for manufacturing processes located in the colonial country. This pattern of mercantilism prevented the colonized countries from developing their own industrialization. But multinational corporations were changing that pattern. Labor costs in areas such as the United States were seen as too expensive to maintain high profits. Multinational corporations were pulling their factories out of the industrial cities of North America and moving them to the Third World in order to take advantage of lower wages, lack of unionization and lack of pollution regulation.

But this internationalization of production only exploited these factors in the Third World for higher profits in order to create products designed for an elite global market. Such new industrialization created few jobs for Third World workers, since it arrived on a capital intensive and high technological level. It also consolidated international control over the modernized sector of the Latin American economy, while displacing native handicrafts, small businesses and subsistence farming. Far from trickling down to the masses of Latin American people, such development created an increasing gap between the rich and the poor. Displaced from traditional means of subsistence in the countryside, but unable to find new employment in the cities, roughly a third or more of the population of Latin American countries were becoming chronically unemployed, forming belts of squatter towns around the glittering modern cities of Mexico City, Buenos Aires or Bogota.

The 1960's and 70's saw efforts at democratic reform snuffed out by military coups. Military national security states emerged, which abolished even the facade of democratic freedoms and human rights. Dissent was repressed by secret armies of internal police, and the torture and "disappearance" of progressive leaders became the order of the day. The United States was a major supporter of these right-wing national security states and their armies of repression. After the Cuban revolution, American aid to Latin America, originally proclaimed as aid to "development," in fact became primarily military aid for these armies of internal repression of dissent. The U.S. Army School of the Americas in the Panama Canal Zone, and other schools, such as Fort Bragg, North Carolina and Fort Leavenworth, Kansas, trained and equipped a new Latin American military force in the ideology and hardware to repress the liberation struggles of their own people. Any kind of autonomous popular movements for self-determination were immediately labeled "communism" by the United States government and its dependent elites, while "defense of democracy" became a slogan that covered up brutal tyranny and sham elections.[9]

This perception of the more radical nature of the crisis of oppressive power and grinding poverty and oppression led many Catholic pastors and theologians to reject the concept of development for that of liberation. Liberation does not mean a rejection of modern technology and industrialization. Rather, it means that the ownership of the means of production must be radically altered. Latin Americans must lead successful revolutions against control of their national resources by foreign governments and companies, and against the Latin American elites who mediate this dependency and who are kept in power by foreign economic and military aid. Self-determination, under regimes that sponsor grassroots democratic-socialist methods of development from the bottom up, is needed to really meet the needs of the Latin American poor.

Beginning in the late 1960's with the work of theologians such as Gustavo Gutierrez, a theology of liberation began to emerge from Latin America to give Christian expression to this new urgency for radical social change.[10] In 1968 at the second meeting of the Latin American Bishops' Conference in Medellin, Colombia, these liberation theologians and their episcopal allies, such as Dom Helder Camera of Racife, Brazil, were able to shape a church document that gave support to this new social commitment of the church to the cause of the poor. The document that emerged from the conference condemned the "international imperialism of money," located the roots of violence in the institutionalized violence of poverty and repression and pledged the church to a struggle on behalf of a new economic order freed from dependency.[11]

In an effort to bridge the gap between the small number of priests and the huge number of the poorly catechized baptized, the bishops also gave support to the idea of Basic Christian Communities. These are small Christian groups for prayer, Bible study and reflection on the ethical implication of committed Christian life. They are generally led by lay catechists, rather than by priests. These base communities quickly were seen by liberation theologians as the popular foundation for a new Christianity committed to the struggle of the poor for social justice.[12]

It was not long before conservative movements, seeking to repress and discredit liberation theology, arose among right-wing bishops and social elites in Latin America, supported by conservatives in the Vatican. The American State Department and CIA also quickly perceived a threat from this new alliance of religion and revolutionary politics. Such an alliance threatened the traditional stereotype of socialists as "godless" materialists, hostile to religious and ethical values.

In 1972 Monsignor Lopez Trujillo, a conservative allied with international as well as Latin American right-wing groups, captured the leadership of the Latin American Bishop's Conference and began to organize conservative and centrist church leaders to discredit liberation theology and repress Basic Christian Communities. Plans were laid for a third bishops' conference in Puebla, Mexico, that would complete this process of repression. Liberation theologians and their episcopal allies were prevented from becoming advisors or delegates to this conference.

But, despite the well-laid plans, Puebla did not succeed in becoming a success for the opponents of liberation theology in the Latin American church and their allies in the Vatican, such as Cardinal Baggio. The preparatory document, prepared in secret by picked allies of Monsignor Trujillo, was leaked to leaders of the popular church movements. As a result, widespread discussion took place among grass-roots communities. Critical responses were sent back to the secretariat in Bogota, as well as being published or circulated popularly.

When the conference finally gathered in January of 1979, representatives of uninvited groups—liberation theologians, sociologists, leaders of popular church movements and even an organized group of feminists—gathered their own popular conference outside the walls of the seminary where the delegates were housed. They managed to generate enough discussion to influence the middle-of-the-road bishops within. The result was a moderate document that reaffirmed most of the basic commitments of Medellin. Liberation theology was not condemned, and base communities were encouraged. The new Pope, John Paul II, appeared to open the conference. But his speeches, which had been intended by Trujillo to give the *coup de grace* to liberation theology, were sufficiently ambivalent to provide fuel for both sides. Particularly his more spontaneous speeches, delivered to Indians and workers, contained strong language of commitment of the church to social justice. The material from the Pope's speeches that made its way into the final document of Puebla consistently quoted his language advocating social justice.[13]

However, the Puebla conference did not end the efforts of conservative Latin American churchmen, and their U.S. and Vatican

allies, to marginalize liberation theologians and to crush a popular
church allied with movements of the poor. This conflict has been
heightened by the victory of the Sandinista revolutionary movement in Nicaragua shortly after the Puebla conference. This was
the first revolutionary government to come to power since the
development of liberation theology and to have been inspired and
aided by these new Christian popular movements. The Cuban revolution of 1959 took place before these developments in a country
where both the Catholic and the Protestant churches were strongly
associated with the colonial powers. There the Marxist government
has followed the traditional line of seeing religion as an antirevolu-
tionary force. Only recently, with greater security and popular economic success of the Cuban revolutionary efforts, as well as the
permeation of liberation Christianity into Cuban Catholicism and
Protestantism, has there been a new rapprochement between the
Cuban revolutionary government and the churches there.[14]

But the Nicaraguan revolution emerged, in part, from popular
Christian movements. It numbers prominent Catholic priests in its
leadership, such as poet Ernesto Cardenal, who was named Minister
of Culture of the revolutionary regime. The policy of the American
government toward the Nicaraguan government has been a con-
certed effort to destroy its popular support, both within the country and abroad. A key part of this effort has been the attempt to
foment a split of conservative church hierarchy from the popular
church and to create an image of the Sandinistas as "persecutors"
of the church, rather than as revolutionaries supported by a popular Christianity.

The Vatican has also cooperated in this effort for its own reasons,
which seem to be primarily a fear of a popular Christianity, no longer
controlled by the hierarchy, and an image of communism shaped
by the Pope's Eastern European experience. Support for increasingly reactionary stances of the archbishop of Managua, Obando
y Bravo, and condemnation of the popular church, have expressed
this Vatican suspicion. The priests who are a part of the Sandinista
government were ordered to resign and, when they refused to do

so, were forced from their religious orders and stripped of the right to exercise their priesthood.[15]

These movements of the Vatican against liberation theology and the popular church have also been expressed in investigations of theologians, such as Leonardo Boff and Gustavo Gutierrez, and in the document prepared by Cardinal Ratzinger, head of the Vatican Congregation of the Faith, that was intended to condemn liberation theology as a heretical politicization of Christianity. Liberation theologians, however, have not been idle in the face of these attacks. Although the Vatican succeeded in imposing a silencing of Leonardo Boff for eleven months, this "silence" only succeeded in focusing attention on his powerful critique of tyrannical church authority in his 1985 volume, *Church, Charism and Power.*[16]

The document prepared by Cardinal Ratzinger to condemn liberation theology was expertly dissected by liberation theologian Juan Luis Segundo, who showed that the presuppositions of the document about Marxism, secularism and the separation of the spiritual and the political have little to do with the foundations of liberation theology. What the Cardinal condemned was not the real liberation theology, but a straw man created in Europe.[17] Important groups of Latin American bishops, especially those from Brazil, moreover, have stepped in to defend their theologians and thus have blunted conservative Vatican efforts to condemn them.[18]

Increasingly, liberation theologians have sharpened their own analysis of the conflict, recognizing that class struggle, the struggle between institutionalized privilege and the poor, does not just divide society, but divides the church as well. There are two fundamentally different kinds of religion or spirituality: a religion that sacralizes oppressive power and unjust wealth, which names its exponents as representatives of God and its system of power as the work and will of God; and a spirituality of conversion to justice, solidarity with the poorest and most oppressed of society, and quest for a new order of human relationships.

Only this second kind of spirituality is authentically biblical, authentically in line with the message of the prophets and of Jesus. The first type of religion is the false religiosity of the Powers and Principalities. It is the religion of the Golden Calf which ever seeks to substitute itself for the religion of the cross. The real conflict over religion is not a conflict between religious belief and atheistic materialism, as the Vatican would have it, but the conflict between authentic biblical faith that does justice, and idolatry, which worships the systems of oppressive power of the world. Pressed by ecclesiastical and political persecution, liberation theology has responded by becoming more profoundly biblical, searching the Scriptures, rather than texts of sociological analysis, for the primary inspiration of their struggle.[19]

This conflict between First and Third World theology, between hierarchical and popular Christianity, also has its expressions in Africa and Asia. Here the question of a popular liberation Christianity, allied with the struggles of the poor for a more just society, is often joined to questions of cultural indigenization. In Latin America the pre-Christian religions of the Indians were effectively smashed and replaced by European Christian culture. Remnants may remain among remote Indian communities, but such traces of earlier religious culture have little influence on theologians trained in European universities. Thus, although Latin Americans speak of a rejection of a European-centered Christianity and the need to contextualize Christianity in Latin America, what they mean primarily is a contextualization in post-colonial Latin American historical experience, rather than in an alternative culture rooted in precolonial, indigenous sources.[20]

The situation is very different in Africa and Asia where Christianity faces strong indigenous religious challenges, from Islam and from traditional African religions, and from highly cultured religious systems, as well as popular expressions, of Hinduism, Buddhism and Taoism. New theologies are also rising among Christians in these regions which seek to break the hegemony of Greco-European culture upon Christian thought, and to incarnate both the theology and the prayer life of Christians in native cultural forms.[21]

In the last ten years (since 1976) there has also emerged a dialogue between Third World theologians of Asia, Africa and Latin America. These dialogues have been organized through the international network, the Ecumenical Association of Third World Theologians (EAWOT). These meetings, at first, found Third World theologians divided over the competing agendas of liberation and cultural indigenization. But it has become apparent that these two agendas must go hand in hand. There is not one, but many, Third World theologies. Christianity must both situate itself culturally, and find its ethical task on behalf of social justice, in a variety of different regions. These regions have distinct cultures and socioeconomic issues in relationship to the neocolonial powers, as well as to the local elites.

What all Third World theologies and religious movements signify, however, is a decisive break with Western European ethnocentrism. Christianity can no longer be identified with the expansion of Western civilization. Rome, or Western European theological faculties, can no longer presume that they are the centers for defining global Christianity. Christian churches in Latin America, Asia and Africa are emerging as subjects of their own self-definition, not simply objects of definition and control from outside. They are demanding both ecclesial and intellectual autonomy, autonomy to govern their own churches, and autonomy to define their own theological perspectives. European or North American churches can be in communion with the churches in the Third World only by recognizing them as peers in a dialogue of equals. They are no longer the masters in relation to culturally inferior subjects.

This emergence of the Third World takes place at a time of significant demographic shifts in the Catholic and Christian population of the world. The Reformation of the sixteenth century, and the identification of Protestantism with industrialized countries, such as England and the United States, was once taken as proof that

Protestantism represents the *avant garde* of "liberty, progress and modern times," while Catholicism was the dominant religion only in retrograde areas, such as Italy and Ireland. But this identification of Catholicism with the marginal populations of Europe—Poles, Irish and Latins—today begins to acquire a different meaning. It means a Catholicism whose popular base is more in the populations pushed aside or exploited by capitalist industrialization, rather than those who have been its primary beneficiaries.

This social location of Catholicism among the less privileged acquires deeper significance in a global context. Here the fastest growing Catholic population is to be found among Hispanics who will soon outnumber Catholics of European background, even in the United States. Africa also has a fast-growing Christian population, both Catholic and Protestant, who have the enthusiasm of new converts for their religion. In a given Sunday in Accra, the capital of Ghana, some 65% of the population can be found in church, in contrast to 10-12 percent in Rome, London or Paris. Thus, in the future, the bulk of the Christian population of the world will be black, brown or yellow rather than white, poor rather than affluent, and on the revolutionary side of struggles over global military and economic power.

These shifts in the base of the Catholic and Christian population to the Third World, and the emerging consciousness of Third World Christians, will make it more, rather than less, difficult for the Catholic Church to continue to operate as the ecclesiastical arm of ruling classes of the world, whether based in Western Europe or North America. Within a remarkably short time the new consciousness that began to take expression in the late sixties is transforming the theology and practice of Third World Christians. Reversing colonial relations, this new consciousness is now evangelizing the churches of Europe and North America. If one were to look for prophetic leaders among contemporary churchmen, one would more likely name Helder Camera of Brazil, Ernesto Cardenal of Nicaragua or Desmond Tutu of South Africa, than any figure emerging from the white First World.

Returned missionaries have also played an important role in bringing this prophetic consciousness of Third World Christianity back
to the First World churches. The key to this new consciousness is
summed up in the phrase "preferential option for the poor." This
option for the poor is not to be understood as mere charitable out-
reach to the poor by the affluent. It is not, first of all, we, the
affluent, who opt for the poor. Rather, according to liberation theologians, it is God who opts for the poor throughout history, summed
up in the life of Jesus Christ. God's option for the poor stands as
a judgment against our unjust wealth and power. Conversion to the
gospel means a repentant shift in the basis of our social identification as the Christian church. It means following Christ's identification with the poor by seeking to transform social structures and
relationships which generate deprivation and dehumanization. For
Salvadoran theologian Jon Sobrino this redefines the fundamental meaning and criteria for recognizing the "true church." Only a
church committed to the poor, on behalf of a just human community, can today be regarded as the authentic church of Jesus
Christ.[22]

The challenge of the Third World calls for a church that starts at
the base, identified with the poorest, rather than with those in
power. The revolution it seeks is not one that would simply upend
the pyramid, creating a new class of oppressors from those presently
poor, but a society in which justice and love are really and practically incarnate. This may never happen finally or perfectly, but the
Christian must seek constantly better approximations of the just
and loving society. Thus liberation can never be identified simply
with ideologies (or theologies) about liberation, nor can it be
assumed to be the assured possession of any particular social system. Rather, prophetic critique must be based on constant discern-
ment of the realities of the "signs of the times." We must ask about
what is actually happening, not just discuss theoretical constructs
divorced from reality.

This vision of the church in repentant and practical solidarity with
the poor, on behalf of a more just society for all, deeply divides

Catholicism, both in Latin American and in the global church. Vatican retrenchment that directs its attacks against liberation theologians and the popular church movements of the Third World, reflects this challenge. Constant admonitions from Vatican conservatives to avoid "Marxist analysis" and to reject political involvement by priests, reflect a church fearful of losing its place in the seats of power.

A church on the side of the powerful wishes to extend charity to the poor, but not to stand with them in a way that would be in conflict with the interests of economic and military elites. This is the real meaning of the hostility of churchmen to "class analysis" and "class struggle," and not, as they would contend, their desire to spread "love" and acceptance around equally to all classes. In a world divided by institutionalized violence and oppression, the only way to love one's neighbor is to stand with the poor and to seek to dismantle the systems of privilege. To love the rich means to stand in judgment on their unjust wealth. Reconciliation is possible only on the basis of repentance and transformation that incarnates new social relations between people in society.

In a polarized world of vast wealth and grinding poverty, threatened with nuclear annihilation as the final defense against social transformation, class conflict is not a theory with which one agrees or does not agree. It is the social reality in which we all live. Not to choose the side of the poor is to choose the side of the affluent. There is no theology that can be socially neutral or "purely spiritual." Those who choose the side of the poor must also know that they make themselves the marked target of those in power. This is evident for the missionaries who have committed themselves to the poor of Guatemala or El Salvador, for example. To opt for the poor is to lose one's place among the powerful, to choose vulnerability, poverty, perhaps torture and death. It is to choose to follow in the footsteps of Jesus Christ by becoming a martyr church.

In Latin America the church which opts for the poor is learning anew what it means to be baptized into the death and resurrection of Christ. The cross has ceased to be a gold and jeweled artifact hanging on a church wall. It has become the living reality that Christians bear in their own bodies. The cry of *"presenté"*, by which the Latin American popular church remembers its martyrs, is the concrete, living expression of the presence of the Risen Lord. This is the witness of the Latin American and Third World churches to the churches of residual Euro-American Christendom.

The churches and theological faculties of the First World would like to have it both ways. We would like to entertain Third World liberation theologians as "stars" of a new "field" of theology and to bring them to give invitational lectures to prove that we are *au courant*. But liberation theologians, rightly, seek to avoid that cooptation into a new intellectual elite. As Gustavo Gutierrez repeatedly has said, "the subject of liberation theology is not theology, but liberation." The criteria lie the reality of *praxis*, not theory about *praxis*. The critical question is not whether you have the right words, but rather how you commit your life.

"Which side are you on?" is the challenge of the Third World church to those who profess to be Christians among the powerful. Only when that commitment is clear and efficacious is it worth talking about how to avoid violence and how to bring compassion and reconciliation to the process of revolutionary transformation of social relationships. The future of Catholicism in the world today rests very much on how it responds to this revolutionary challenge from Third World people, both within and outside the Christian fold. Will it choose to stand with a new future for all, through solidarity with the poor, or will it fall back upon its traditional alliances with the ruling classes?

CHAPTER 4
WHAT IS TO BE DONE

Many Catholics in recent years have found the resistance of the hierarchy to these challenges offered by liberalism, feminism and Third World liberation movements so discouraging, their own position in the Catholic Church so untenable and expectations of change from the top so unlikely, that they ask "why bother with the Catholic Church at all?" Isn't the effort to work within it simply helping to perpetuate a bad system? Why not get out of it and work for change in secular society? Such questions cannot be taken lightly. They are asked from a profound experience of existential despair.

Some feminists suspect a kind of masochism in their own or other women's continued defense of remaining "in" a church which continually marginalizes and insults them. As Mary Jo Weaver, author of the recent book on contemporary Catholic feminism, has put it on several occasions, we need to know that the Catholic hierarchy "doesn't want us, has never wanted us and never will want us."[1] What is it then that *we want* when we continue to hang around an institution that they govern?

63

In the last year, two ordained women, one an Anglican priest and another a Methodist minister, both of them lesbians, have suggested to me that they, and I, are like battered wives. The same analogy has occurred to Catholic nuns who have compared themselves to battered wives in relation to the Sacred Congregation of Religious and Secular Institutes, which claims ultimate jurisdiction over them. Our reasons for "staying in the church" sound like the same excuses that battered wives give for not leaving a battering husband. "He didn't really mean it." "He really loves me." "He is trying to change." "He needs me in order to change." None of these excuses will wash.

This analogy between battered wives and Christian women who can't manage to break our attachment to patriarchal church leaders has some truth in it. But the analogy is perhaps not exact. We need to get out of any immediate situation that batters us. Violence, whether to the spirit or to the body, should not be tolerated for any "good cause," and we are unlikely to be able to serve any good cause by tolerating it. But it is one thing to get out of the domestic situation that is battering you and another thing to recognize that you are still part of the same society with the batterer. That recognition calls not only for an exodus from personal battering, but also for a response that constructs shelters for the battered to flee into and seeks laws and community action to restrain the batterers. It is this second task that we should be about in the church.

The larger and more important question is whether there is spiritual validity in the Christian church and, specifically, in its Roman Catholic expression at all. Why claim this institution as the society in which to live? For me the answer to this question goes to the very heart of the relationship between God/ess (or ultimate truthful and good reality) and human sin (failure to live in harmony with the ultimate truthful and good reality).

When one looks at the Roman Catholic Church throughout its long history, and even today, what one sees, from one vantage point, is a scandalous record of power-mongering. These are not accidental, "private" sins of individuals. They flow out of the ideology and collective organization of hierarchical, patriarchal clericalism. As such, the Roman Catholic Church is an outrageous institution undeserving of our loyalty.

Looked at from another vantage point, the Roman Catholic Church is a vast diverse network of more than 627 million people around the world in all cultures and walks of life, struggling to be faithful and to make sense of their lives. Such a vast network of people cannot be ignored. At the minimum it deserves to have a better faith, better hopes, better love. Thus when we speak of remaining "in" the church, we need to be clear about what exactly we remain "in" and what we are loyal to. My relationship is one of solidarity with that vast human community in need, to which I have some special, but not exclusive, responsibility. My loyalty is to the Good News of Jesus Christ which, despite all the poor service it has received from its institutional representatives, still contains for me the key to that better faith, hope and love. Loyalty then needs to be to people and to the gospel. Institutions should be called to become servants of the people through the gospel, instead of seeking to substitute themselves for the community and for the Holy One and trying to make themselves the object of our loyalty.

The gospel of forgiveness of sins makes it possible continually to get our priorities right and to refuse to take the idolatrous pretenses of the institutions as seriously as they would like to be taken. This means not only that we do not confuse their idols with the true Holy One, but also that we are not so ultimately horrified and angry at their sinfulness that we fail to notice that these idols are masks behind which hides a pathetic, insecure creature. Like Dorothy in Oz, we have pulled back the curtain that hides the Wizard and have seen that the thunderous image of authority is a fake projected on a screen by a funny little man cranking away at his mummery machine. Like Dorothy, we cry out in dismay, "You are a very bad man!" The Wizard, if he were capable of being truthful, should reply sadly, "No, my dear, I am not a *very* bad man. I am just a very bad wizard."

This is not to say that sin is not real and serious. The church's bad imitations of deity down through the centuries have caused uncountable evils of misery, violence, slaughter, lies, hatred and despair. Such affrontry against the real Divine One deserves all the denunciatory wrath of Biblical prophets. But this judgmental wrath stands in the larger context of a divine mercy that does not dehumanize even the ones who have most dehumanized themselves. Behind the wrathful visage of divine anger so richly deserved, one must see perhaps a kind of puzzled sorrow at the pathetic weakness of creatures who are so faithless that they think they need infallible popes and inerrant Bibles.

Assuming then a community of people who have the gospel of Jesus Christ as a context of meaning in their lives and this particular network of people, gathered by Roman Catholic culture and institutions, as a special, but not exclusive, human concern, what is to be done? How can we, that is, those concerned with intellectual freedom and social justice in this particular church community, both provide ourselves with the religious nurture and means of action that we need and also continue to work to make changes in its historical institutions?

I believe that the first question we need to ask is not what we should do "for the church," but what we should do for ourselves. What is it that we need to nurture and express in our Christian vision? I invite anyone reading this book to stop at this point and reflect on their own answer to that question. What do I need from a community of faith? Make a list of those needs and then compare them with the reality of the church communities available to you. What does this church actually offer to you as usable vehicles for responding to these needs? What should it be offering?

What kind of liturgical community would make weekly worship a feast for the soul, an occasion to be eagerly anticipated, rather than, as it so often has been, a barely tolerable duty? (Is this why the pre-Vatican II church tried to pretend it was a mortal sin if one missed Sunday Mass? Did they actually assume that no one would come unless threatened by hellfire and damnation?) What kind of ministry do we need to support our personal, moral and spiritual development, in community with others? What kind of ministry do we feel called to exercise and what would make that possible? What do we think the church should be about in the world? Which of these things is it possible to do or to have in the local parishes to which you have access? In religious orders? In other institutional means, such as retreat centers?

If it becomes evident through this self-examination that the institutional church has put insurmountable obstacles in the way of even beginning to ask, much less answer, these questions, then it is time for us to invent new means of spiritual community, celebration and action. This does not mean neglecting to ask how we can make use of existing means as well. Our starting point must be a claiming of ourselves as church. This means that we know that we are empowered by the Holy Spirit, as the people of Christ, to create for ourselves the expressions of worshipping community and ministry that we need. This power cannot be alienated from us by any ecclesiastical hierarchy.

The Italian Basic Christian Community Movement calls this starting point "reappropriation theology."[2] We reappropriate the ministry of Word, sacrament and service falsely alienated from the people by the ecclesiastical ruling class. Reappropriation theology means a basic spiritual revolution in our consciousness that puts our lives, as the community, at the center of the meaning of being church, rather than seeing ourselves at the periphery, banging on locked doors, ever asking for permission to breathe from those we imagine own the conduits of the Spirit.

Once we have reappropriated our spiritual power, then we can be about forming base communities for whatever we want and feel called to do. These might be base communities for worship, for consciousness-raising and mutual support; for study and discussion; peace and justice centers to express our *praxis* in society; specialized ministries to respond to particular needs such as reproductive rights, or homeless women and children, or refugees menaced by deportation, or solidarity with Third World oppressed communities such as Central America or South Africa. Some may wish to go farther and form more total communities for living together, worship and ministry—perhaps new kinds of religious orders, not under patriarchal control.

This new community-building impulse is found in many places around the world, among Catholics and other Christians and in other religious traditions, such as the Havurah movement among renewal-minded American Jews.[3] There needs to be more networking for exchange of ideas among these various kinds of base community movements. These include the base communities of Latin America and Africa which have become a base for the living of liberation theology. They include the network of European base communities in Italy, Holland and elsewhere. The European base communities particularly have brought together concerns for peace and nuclear disarmament, for workers and racial minorities in their midst and for women's issues in the society and the churches.[4]

Increasingly, a concern for a feminist focus has emerged as central to gatherings of Christian women who realize that not only are they marginalized in the official churches, but their concerns are also marginalized in gatherings of leftist men who are concerned with all kinds of abstract categories of oppression except those which concretely and specifically affect women. Networks of feminist theology and worship have sprung up in Europe, England and the United States, and probably elsewhere as well. In England the Women in Theology group and the Catholic Women's Network gather Christian feminist women together for lectures, reflection and worship. In the United States feminist worship gatherings have greatly proliferated in major urban areas. Among Catholics this movement is networked through a group of Catholic feminist organizations called the Women of the Church Convergence. The name "Women-church" has been taken as the way of claiming the power to be church now for Catholic women.[5]

For many people the mention of such networks may make them feel that this is a special clique that either excludes them or to which they have no access. Thus it is necessary to demystify the "otherness" of such small groups. All of them started by a couple of people getting together in a living room, an office, a restaurant, a chaplaincy or whatever and saying "what do we need and how can we start doing it together?" Any two or three gathered together can do the same.

Once we have begun to meet some of our own needs for supportive community, worship and action, then we can start to ask how can or should such Christian base communities relate to the historical institutions. Although such a reappropriation of our own spiritual power and community-building capacities may seem like the exact opposite of remaining "in" or concerned about the reform of historical institutions, such as the Roman Catholic Church, I would suggest that it is actually the only basis on which many of us can continue to do so. Only when we are no longer operating from a position of emptiness, frustration, anger, loneliness and mental and spiritual exhaustion, when we are no longer making the struggle with unresponsive institutional systems the primary context of our relationship to "the church," will we be liberated enough to address, with maturity, objectivity and compassion, the problems of making this ancient juggernaut called the Roman Catholic Church a somewhat better vehicle for faith, hope and love.

Why should we be concerned to make this institution function better if we are already "doing our thing?" Why don't we just bring together the network of our base communities, peace and justice organizations and study groups and call it the "new church"? It is at this point that I think that Catholic liberal-leftists need to gain greater respect for and understanding of the function of historical institutions. We tend to assume that if only we, the critical ones, disaffiliate from the Roman Catholic Church, it will dry up and disappear. We fail to appreciate how much we are actually dependent on institutional networks of communication which we do not sustain with our personal resources. The impact of our critique is enormously magnified precisely because it lays hold, in some way or another, of vehicles of communication sustained by this larger system.

Canadian theologian Gregory Baum once compared the church to a telephone system.[6] We notice the vehicle itself only when it doesn't work, when it blocks our efforts to communicate. We generally don't realize the enormous maintenance work that goes into creating such a system, when it does work and when we are using it to talk to someone else in a distant place. Because we don't understand and respect the millions of invisible links that connect us with each other, Catholics easily become naive anarchists. We forget that, no matter how great our living room liturgy may be, or how much useful work our battered women's shelter may be doing, our own resources can only sustain these efforts for a few years. One needs to look to larger social systems to give these efforts more ongoing life and meaning.

We should be clear that the parish will go on, whether we are worshipping there or not, and will probably not even notice our absence. Whether we are there or not, the parish will continue to be the main vehicle for gathering and socializing the Catholic people throughout the world and down through the generations. Unless we manage to insert what we are doing in a more autonomous setting back into some communication hookup with these main institutional vehicles of ministry and community, breathing new life and activity into them by sharing our ideas and work with people who gather there, our projects will have little lasting impact.

I see church reform as a dialectical process, a constant welling up of new movements of the Spirit which express themselves in small intentional groups gathered to express new visions and needs, and the constant gathering in of these new movements into the institutional church. In this way the institutional church itself is given new life, but also the institutional church gives lasting historical impact to these new movements of the Spirit.

Institutional church leaders have always felt threatened by new movements of the Spirit outside their control. They have always sought to marginalize and stifle them, and so the new movements have tended either to give up or to get mad and go away and found another church which, in turn, becomes another historical institution resistant to new movements for change. Thus do schisms and denominations proliferate in the history of Christianity. Although I am not totally against forming new churches, what is clear to me is that forming new churches never did much to reform the church that you left. It is precisely reforming this particular historical institution that concerns me.

This concerns me for two reasons. First, I believe it will continue to be around and even to grow, particularly in the Third World, whether we stick with it or not. Second, I think that, through a series of historical accidents, the Catholic Church today finds itself in a unique position of being a major global institution that links the communist, the capitalist and the Third Worlds. It is, therefore, in a critical position to bridge these three worlds and to witness to the needs of our planet for peace and justice. So it seems to me extremely important that critical and justice-minded minorities stay in this church and use whatever parts of it they can get their hands on to respond appropriately to these critical challenges of human survival.

Moreover, these critical minorities will have far more impact both on the church and on the world if they continue to find ways to work through or impact its institutions, than they could possibly have if they separated from it. One should only think of how few are the liberation theologians of Latin America and yet what an enormous impact they have already had, precisely because what they do is broadcast through this global network called the Roman Catholic Church. This is like the difference between shouting with the unaided human voice and speaking through a global system of telecommunications. This means we need to figure out how to use institutional networks creatively, rather than feeling powerless before them.

We can do this by creating new vehicles of ministry, community and communication, and then "attaching" them to the edges of the existing historical church, so they become new vehicles within and for the whole Catholic community. American Catholicism has been particularly adept at doing this. Almost all of the most lively expressions of American Catholicism come from new initiatives, developed either by religious orders or by laity, which operate autonomously or quasi-autonomously from the hierarchy but nevertheless function as expressions of the Catholic community. One has only to think of the Catholic Worker Movement; the Catholic colleges, increasingly today under lay boards; the independent Catholic press; the network of Peace and Justice centers; the networks of Catholic women, both religious and lay, such as the National Association of Religious Women and Chicago Catholic Women; Catholic advocacy groups of various kinds, such as Dignity, Catholics for a Free Choice and the Association for the Rights of Catholics in the Church, not to mention the Chicago Call to Action.

One failing of these parallel groups is a tendency to get too separated from the ordinary vehicles of Catholic life, particularly the parish. Whenever possible, one should use these ordinary structures for such activities (although, if this is blocked, one should not hesitate to meet in other structures, while still calling oneself Catholic). If one has a liberation or feminist theology lecture series, one should try to hold it in a Catholic college or parish. If you are producing a new newspaper, you should try to distribute it in parishes. If you have a study group that is open to new members, one should advertise it in the parish bulletin. It is in this way that new initiatives interpenetrate and renew ordinary Catholic life, and also that we stay in touch with ordinary Catholic life and do not imagine that it is better or worse than it actually is.

It used to be said, with some irony, that the laity in the Catholic Church had no power to govern or make decisions. Their role was to "pay, pray and obey." What was not recognized was what enormous power that gave the laity if we stopped "paying, praying and obeying" as we are told. Through base communities and intentional worship groups we are learning to pray anew, in words that we choose and which mediate the presence and healing power of the Holy One for us. We are also claiming our own consciences, and are no longer willing to give "blind obedience" to decrees that conflict with our own experience and moral integrity. This withdrawal of obedience should by no means be seen as an arbitrary, individualistic process, without authentic testing in the conscience of the Catholic community. Rather, what Catholics are recognizing is that the episcopal magisterium is only one of the sources of authority, among others. When it refuses to test its own teaching by consultation with moral and scriptural theologians, social experts and the experience of the people, it swings off-base and loses its credibility.

The alternative consensus on birth control that emerged in the late 1960's, represents an authentic model of consultation between theological and social experts and grass-roots experience of Catholics serious about their moral lives. It was the Pope, not the people, who chose to dissent from the consensus of the church in 1968 when he issued *Humanae Vitae*. We need to be serious about shaping the kind of consultation with all the sources of authority— Scripture and tradition, theological and social experts and the experience of the people—from which credible teaching can emerge. It is then the job of the hierarchy to enunciate, not to originate, this consensus of the church. They should do this modestly, as a "working consensus" that is open to the critical voice, which may not yet be widely understood but which may be the harbinger of a larger truth.

Finally, the third area of power that the Catholic laity can and should take into their hands is the decision to pay, how much and to whom. This means not simply to demand accountability for what we have paid to official church organs, although this too is appropriate. We should pay into funds in our parishes and dioceses that will actually go to serving the poor and to creating a more just world. We should withdraw payment from ecclesiastical funds that seek to stifle our vision and to repress a widening ministry. This means, at times, that we need to invent new funds of our own and divert our giving into the sort of pastoral and social work that is more truly lifegiving.

Catholic feminist groups have been active for some years in using the power of the "women's mite" in this way. For several years women's groups supporting women's ordination deposited wooden nickels or Susan B. Anthony dollars into the collection plate on the Sunday that the collection was taken for diocesan seminaries. These protest symbols said that we do not support a patriarchal church that discriminated against women and that our money had gone to an alternative fund to support women's theological education. Even if each pastor got only one or two of these communications, it would be hard to miss the point!

Recently, Chicago Catholic women have developed an alternative fund called "Mary's Pence." This fund will provide an alternative to the annual Peter's Pence that goes to support the Vatican. It will be used to support ministries by and for women. By taking hold of our own powers, the powers to pray, to pay and to obey, we confront the hierarchical church with a challenge it cannot well ignore, but also which it cannot stifle or control. If many Catholics start deciding how they will pray, pay and obey, the hierarchical church will lose the capacity to govern unilaterally. It will be forced to come to terms with a more participatory church, a more participatory church which we are already creating at the base. These suggestions about "what is to be done" are not definitive or adequate. Many new, inventive voices need to be added to this discussion. But perhaps they indicate that there are ways forward. One does not have to feel paralyzed by a helpless feeling that the "captains" of the ship have set their course in a direction opposite to the one we wish to go and that we are powerless to do anything about it, that we have no alternative but to jump overboard alone or perhaps organize small groups to seize the life rafts.

The challenges to the Catholic Church at this time in history are great. It perhaps has a unique opportunity, as not since its early formative centuries when the Roman Empire was collapsing, to give a positive Christian witness that could be salvific for much of humanity. But it may fail to rise to the occasion and may regress into a reactionary stance that simply seeks to repress the challenges of intellectual and institutional freedom, mature sexual morality, justice for women and for homosexuals and service to the poor. Whether or not the creative and critical groups in its midst choose to find ways to use this historical community, to impact and shape it and to express their best hopes through it, will make the difference between whether it rises to this occasion or loses this opportunity to become a sign of the good news.

Notes

Introduction

1. *Enchiridion Symbolorum Definitionum et Declarationum de Rebus Fidei et Morum*, Henricus Denzinger, ed. (Roma: Herder, 1963), (2901-2980), 576-584.
2. Jay P. Dolan, *The American Catholic Experience: A History from Colonial Times to the Present* (New York: Doubleday, 1985), 96-7.
3. *Ibid.* 105-112.
4. From the *Handbook for Parishioners of the Archdiocese of Milwaukee* 23-24, quoted in Dolan, *op. cit.*, 180-181.
5. Dolan, *ibid.* 296, 206-311.
6. *Ibid.*, 315-319.
7. *Ibid.*, 163-189.
8. *Commonweal* was founded in 1923 and *Cross Currents* in 1950.
9. John Courtney Murray, *We Hold These Truths: Catholic Reflections on the American Proposition* (London: Sheed and Ward, 1961.)
10. *Dogmatic Constitution on the Church (Lumen Gentium)* 9-17, in *The Documents of Vatican II*, Walter M. Abbott, S.J., ed. (London: G. Chapman, 1967), 24-37.
11. The numbers of American women in religious orders declined from 181,421 in 1966 to 126,517 in 1980.
12. Anita Caspary, IHM, "The California IHMs' Story," in *Fidelity in Creating the Future* (Detroit, Michigan: Groundwork for a Just World, 1984), pp. 38-40.
13. Daniel Berrigan, *Block Island* (Greensboro, N.C.: Unicorn Press, 1985).
14. Renny Golden and Michael McConnell, *Sanctuary: The New Underground Railroad* (Maryknoll, N.Y.: Orbis Press, 1986).
15. "This Land Is Home To Me: A Pastoral Letter on Powerlessness in Appalachia," by the Catholic Bishops of the Region (Published by the Catholic Committee of Appalachia, February 1, 1975).
16. "The Challenge of Peace: God's Promise and our Response: A Pastoral Letter on War and Peace," National Conference of Catholic Bishops, May 3, 1983.
17. Third Draft, "Economic Justice for All: Catholic Social Teachings and the U.S. Economy," *Origins* (National Catholic Documentary Service), June 5, 1986 (vol. 16, no. 3).
18. Dolan, *op. cit.*, 443.
19. *Contraception and Holiness: The Catholic Predicament.* Introduction, Archbishop Thomas D. Roberts, S.J. (New York: Herder and Herder, 1964); *What Modern Catholics Think of Birth Control*, William Birmingham, ed. (New York: New American Library, 1964).
20. Robert Blair Kaiser, *The Politics of Sex and Religion: A Case History in the Development of Doctrine, 1962-1984* (Kansas City, MO: Leaven Press, 1985).
21. George Kelly, *The Battle for the American Church* New York: Doubleday, 1979), 188. Also Dolan, *op. cit.*, 435.
22. Andrew Greeley, *The American Catholic* (New York: Basic Books, 1977), 142-150.
23. "The Church, in the Word of God, Celebrates the Mysteries of Christ for the Salvation of the World," December 9, 1985, in *The National Catholic Reporter*, December 20, 1985 (vol. 22, no. 9), 9, 13-16.

Chapter One

1. Ambrose, Letter LI to Theodosius, in *Readings in Church History: From Pente-
cost to the Protestant Revolt*, vol. 1, Colman J. Barry, ed. (Westminster, Maryland:
Westminster Press, 1965), pp. 119-120; S.L. Greenslade, *Church and State from
Constantine to Theodosius* (London: SCM Press, 1954).
2. Ernst Benz, *The Eastern Orthodox Church: Its Thought and Life* (Garden City,
New York: Doubleday, 1963), 163-174.
3. See Brian Tierney, *The Crisis of Church and State 1050-1300* (Englewood Cliffs,
N.J.: Prentice-Hall, 1964); also E.A. Goerner, *Peter and Caesar: Political
Authority and the Catholic Church* (New York: Herder and Herder, 1965).
4. Alec Vidler, *The Church in an Age of Revolution* (Baltimore, Maryland: Pen-
guin Books, 1961), 14-18.
5. *Ibid.*, 18-21.
6. Alec Vidler, *Prophecy and Papacy: A Study of Lamennais, the Church and the
Revolution* (London: SCM Press, 1959).
7. Henry Denzinger, *The Sources of Catholic Dogma*, Roy Deferrari, trans. (New
York: B. Herder Book Co.), 433-442. Vidler, *The Church in an Age of Revolution*, 146-156.
8. Vidler, *Ibid.*, 154-5.
9. One thousand eighty four bishops were eligible to be members of the First Vatican Council. Only 700 were present for the first vote on July 13, 1870 and of
these only 451 voted yes on the doctrine of infallibility. By July 17, 1870, many
of these bishops had left Rome or boycotted the session. Fifty-five continued
to vote *non placet*. On the final vote on July 18, the vote was 533 for and two
against the doctrine. See August Bernhard Hasler, *How the Pope Became Infallible)* Garden City, New York: Doubleday, 1981).
10. Richard Webster, *The Cross and the Fasces: Christian Democracy and Fascism
in Italy* (Stanford, California: Stanford University Press, 1960), 50-106.
11. "The Lateran Pacts of 1929," in John Pollard, *The Vatican and Italian Fascism,
1929-1932* (Cambridge, England: Cambridge University Press, 1985), 197-215.
12. Webster, *op. cit.*, 29, 109.
13. Guenter Lewy, *The Catholic Church and Nazi Germany* (New York: McGraw-
Hill, 1965), 57-93.
14. The play by Rolf Hochhuth, *The Deputy*, focused debate on the issue of Pius
XII's relation to the Jews in the early 1960's.
15. See Pollard's assessment of the compatibility of Catholicism and fascism, *op.
cit.*, 167-194.
16. Webster, *op. cit.*, 178-190.
17. *The Washington Post*, April 12, 1963.
18. *Pacem in Terris:* Encyclical Letter of Pope John XXIII, April 11, 1963 (Washington, DC: National Catholic Welfare Conference, 1963).
19. John Courtney Murray, S.J., "Introduction to the Declaration on Religious Freedom, Vatican II," in *The Documents of Vatican II*, Walter Abbott, S.J., ed. (New
York: America Press, 1966), 672-674.
20. Canadian Bishops' statement: "Christian Ethics and the Economy," in G. Baum
and Duncan Cameron, *Ethics and Economics: Canada's Catholic Bishops on
the Economic Crisis* (Toronto: J. Lorimer, 1984).

21. Joseph Comblin, *The Church and the National Security State* (Maryknoll, NY: Orbis Press, 1979).
22. Peter Hebblethwaite, *The New Inquisition: The Case of Edward Schillebeeckx and Hans Küng* (San Francisco: Harper and Row, 1980).
23. *Authority, Community and Conflict*, Madonna Kolbenschlag, ed. (Kansas City, MO: Sheed and Ward, 1986).
24. Association for the Rights of Catholics in the Church: Charter of Rights, P.O. Box 3932, Philadelphia, PA 19146. Sheed and Ward of Kansas City, MO, will publish a handbook on the charter in the Spring of 1987.
25. Hans Kung, *Infallible? An Inquiry* (Garden City, New York: Doubleday, 1971).

Chapter Two

1. Raphael Patai, *The Hebrew Goddess* (Philadelphia, PA: Ktav Publishing House, 1967), 246-269.
2. William E. Phipps, *Was Jesus Married? The Distortion of Sexuality in the Christian Tradition* (New York: Harper and Row, 1970), 34-98.
3. I Cor. 7, 1-40.
4. I Tim. 2, 14-15.
4. "The Acts of Paul and Thecla," vol. 8 in *Ante-Nicene Fathers*, ed. Alexander Roberts and James Donaldson (New York: Scribners, 1885-1897), 487ff; see also Denis R. MacDonald, *The Legend and the Apostle: The Battle for Paul in Story and Canon* (Philadelphia: Westminister, 1983).
6. Samuel Laeuchli, *Power and Sexuality: The Emergence of Canon Law at the Council of Elvira* (Philadelphia: Temple University Press, 1972).
7. Susan Wemple, *Women in Frankish Society: Marriage and the Cloister, 500-900 A.D.* (Philadelphia: University of Pennsylvania Press, 1983).
8. Carol Karlsen, *The Devil in the Shape of a Woman* (Ph.D Dissertation, Yale University, 1980).
9. John Boswell, *Christianity, Social Tolerance and Homosexuality* (Chicago, IL: Chicago University Press, 1980).
10. Miriam Chusman, "Women in The Reformation in Strasbourg, 1490-1530," *Archiv fur Reformationgeschichte* 63 (1972).
11. Joyce L. Irwin, *Womanhood in Radical Protestantism, 1525-1675* (New York: Edwin Mellen Press, 1979), 179-187, 200-237.
12. William Gouge, "Of Domesticall Duties" (1962), in Joyce Irwin, *Ibid.*, 86-104.
13. Ruth Liebowitz, "Virgins in the Service of Christ: The Dispute Over an Active Apostolate for Women During the Counter-Reformation" in *Women of Spirit: Female Leadership in the Jewish and Christian Traditions*, Rosemary Ruether and Eleanor McLaughlin, eds. (New York: Simon and Schuster, 1979), 131-152.
14. Rosemary Ruether, "Church and Family in the Medieval and Reformation Periods," *New Blackfriars*, February, 1984, 74-86.
15. The restrictive legislation on laicization is found in the *Code of Canon Law: A Text and Commentary*, James Coriden *et al.*, (N.Y.: Paulist Press, 1985), #291-292.
16. The visitation of American Catholic seminaries by teams responsible to Rome has been going on since 1983. In a letter of clarification of the guidelines for Catholic Education, Archbishop William Baum of the curial Congregation for Catholic Education indicated that the non-ordained should not be in positions

of spiritual formation in Catholic seminaries. The letter also suggested that the non-ordained should not teach the sacred sciences and should not be the majority of the students. The particular concern of this warning seems to be to maintain celibate (male) role modeling for the prospective priest. The letter of clarification was circulated in 1983 to Catholic seminaries, but is not a public document. The above information is derived from confidential interviews with professors at Catholic seminaries. See *National Catholic Reporter*, October 7, 1983, p. 1.

17. The statement mandating "fidelity in marriage and celibacy in singleness" appears in *The Book of Discipline of the United Methodist Church* (Nashville, TN: United Methodist Publishing House, 1984), #430.6, p. 431.

18. One of the most developed reports on Catholic ethics and homosexuality appeared as the report of the task force on Gay/Lesbian Issues of the Commission on Social Justice of the Archdiocese of San Francisco: *Homosexuality and Social Justice*, July, 1982. See also *A Time to Speak: Contemporary Statements From U.S. Catholic Sources on Homosexuality, Gay Ministry and Social Justice*, ed. Robert Nugent and Jeannine Gramick (Mt. Rainier, MD: New Ways Ministry, 1982).

19. Arthur Jones, "Legal Action Against Pedophile Priests Grow as Frustrated and Angry Parents Seek Remedies," *National Catholic Reporter* 21:4-6 (June 7, 1985).

20. *Permanent Deacons in the United States: Guidelines on Their Formation and Ministry* (Washington, DC: United States Catholic Conference, 1985), p. 42, # 113, citing the Code of Canon Law, #1087.

22. At the Anti-Suffrage Convention held in Washington, D.C. on December 7, 1916, a message was read from James Cardinal Gibbons, opposing women's suffrage. This was one of many messages that Cardinal Gibbons delivered between 1911 and 1916 opposing women's suffrage (Sophia Smith Collection: Smith College). However, after women won the vote the Cardinal was quick to adapt to using the Catholic women's vote to support the Bishops' social agenda. See Lorine Getz, "Women Struggle for an American Catholic Identity," in Rosemary Ruether and Rosemary Keller, *Women and Religion in America: 1900-1968* (San Francisco: Harper and Row, 1986), 185-6. Papal opposition to all aspects of the movement for the emancipation of women can be found in Pius XI, *Casti Connubii*, December 31, 1930 (Denzinger, #2247-8).

23. Congregation for the Doctrine of the Faith, "Declaration on the Question of the Adminission of Women to the Ministerial Priesthood," October 15, 1976; see also *Women Priests: A Catholic Commentary on the Vatican Declaration*, Leonard and Arlene Swidler, eds. (New York: Paulist Press, 1977).

24. Rosemary Ruether, "The Liberation of Christology from Patriarchy," *Religion in Intellectual Life*, vol. 2, no. 3 (Spring, 1985), 116-128.

25. Augustine, *Soliloquiorum Libri Duo, PL*, vol. XXXII, cols. 878-880; see Shulamith Shahar, *The Fourth Estate: A History of Women in the Middle Ages* (New York: Methuen, 1983), 69.

26. Augustine, *De Ordine, PL*, vol. XXXII, col. 1000; see Shahar, *op. cit.*, 206.

27. See essays in *Contraception and Holiness: The Catholic Predicament*, Introduction by Archbishop Thomas D. Roberts (New York: Herder and Herder, 1964).

28. Robert Blair Kaiser, *The Politics of Sex and Religion* (Kansas City, MO: Leaven Press, 1985).

29. This quotation is taken from oral reminiscenses by Patty Crowley of the Birth Control Commission meetings. Mrs. Crowley can no longer remember with which Cardinal on the Commission the interchange took place.
30. The condemnation of Hans Kung in 1979 by the Congregation for the Doctrine of the Faith, that denied to the German theologian the right to teach as a Catholic theologian, was occasioned primarily by his book, *Infallible? An Inquiry*, published in German in 1970. Kung had been told to write no more on the subject of infallibility. A breach of this directive was seen as having happened in his introduction to August B. Hasler's book, *Wie der Papst unfehlbar wurde*, published in 1979.
31. Kaiser, *op. cit.*, p. 130.
32. For example, see Joseph T. Gill, "His Eminence's Rhetoric Does No Service to the Pro-Life Movement," *The Wanderer*, vol. 177, no. 1 (January 5, 1984), 4.
33. "Catholic Statement of Pluralism and Abortion," *The New York Times*, October 7, 1984, full-page advertisement.
34. *Authority and Community in Conflict*, Madonna Kolbenschlag, ed. (Kansas City, MO: Sheed and Ward, 1986).
35. Charles E. Curran, "Public Dissent in the Church," *Commonweal*, September 12, 1986, 461-470.

Chapter Three

1. Bartolome de las Casas, *The Tears of the Indians: Being a Historical and True Account of the Cruel Massacres and Slaughter of Above Twenty Millions of Innocent People*, trans. John Phillips (London, n.p., 1656).
2. "Politica," in *The Works of Aristotle*, W.D. Ross, ed. (Oxford: Oxford University Press, 1912), X, 1327b 21 and *passim*.
3. The reading of the cursed son of Ham to be Black African is not found in the original Genesis account but developed in the Talmudic commentaries; see Thomas Gossett, *Race: The History of an Idea in America* (New York: Schocken Books, 1965), 5.
4. See George Dunne, *Generation of Giants: The Story of the Jesuits in China in the Last Decades of the Ming Dynasty* (Notre Dame, University Press, 1962).
5. John Paul II, "Discourse to the Bishops of the Cameroon speaking about Evangelization and Inculturation of Christianity in Africa" (August 13, 1985), *Origins*, no. 36 (September 9, 1985); see *National Catholic Reporter*, August 30, 1985.
6. Both men were examined by the Inquisition before execution: John E. Fagg, *Latin America: A General History* (New York: Macmillan, 1963), 444-446.
7. Youth Organization of the Party of National Action, "Social Justice and Christian Democracy in Mexico," in Frederick B. Pike, *The Conflict Between Church and State in Latin America* (New York: Alfred A. Knopf, 1964), 223.
8. See particularly Eduardo Galeano, *The Open Veins of Latin America: Five Centuries of the Pillage of a Continent* (New York: Monthly Review Press, 1973).
9. See particularly the account of U.S. involvement in Central America in Philip Berryman, *The Religious Roots of Rebellion: Christians in the Central America Revolution* (Maryknoll, N.Y.: Orbis Books, 1984), 33-50; also Walter La Feber, *Inevitable Revolutions: The United States in Central America* (New York: W.W. Norton, 1983).

10. Gustavo Gutierrez, *A Theology of Liberation: History, Politics and Salvation* (Maryknoll, NY: Orbis Books, 1973); original Spanish, 1971.
11. *The Church in the Presesnt Day Transformation of Latin America in the Light of the Council:* Final document of the Second General Conference of Latin American Bishops (Bogota, Colombia: General Secretariat of CELAM, 1970).
12. See particularly Leonardo Boff, *Ecclesiogenesis: The Base Communities Re-Invent the Church* (Maryknoll, NY: Orbis Books, 1986); also Sergio Torres and John Eagleson, ed., *The Challenge of Basic Christian Communities* (Maryknoll, NY: Orbis Books, 1982).
13. See the volume edited by John Eagleson and Philip Scharper, *Puebla and Beyond: Documentation and Commentary* (Maryknoll, NY: Orbis Books, 1979).
14. Rosemary Ruether, "Christians and Cubans: A Renewal of Faith," *Christinaity and Crisis*, 45:13 (August 26, 1985), 329-333.
15. Berryman, *op. cit.*, 226-276.
16. Leonardo Boff, *Church, Charism and Power: Liberation Theology and the Institutional Church* (New York: Crossroads, 1986).
17. Joan Luis Segundo, *Theology and the Church: A Response to Cardinal Ratzinger* (Minneapolis, MN: Winston-Salem, 1985).
18. Peter Hebblethwaite, "Lifting of Boff's Silence May Show Move to Curb Ratzinger's Power," *National Catholic Reporter* 22:1 (April 11, 1986).
19. Pablo Richard, *et al.*, *The Idols of Death and the God of Life: A Theology* (Maryknoll, NY: Orbis Books, 1976).
20. Enrique Dussel, *A History of the Church in Latin America: Colonialism to Liberation* (Grand Rapids, MI: William Eerdmans Publishing Company, 1981).

Chapter Four

1. These remarks were made by Mary Jo Weaver at the February 16, 1986 Conference on Women-Church, sponsored by the National Assembly of Religious Women in Chicago, Illinois.
2. This concept of reappropriation theology was laid out by Giovanni Franzoni in a seminar on Christian-Marxist Dialogue held at the Waldensian Seminary in Rome, Italy, March, 1980. See Giovanni Franzoni, *Le Communita di base, Per la riappropriazione della parola di Dio, dei gesti sacramentali, dei ministeri, dell'autonomia politica dei credenti* (Genoa: Lanterna, 1975).
3. Arthur Waskow, *These Holy Sparks: The Rebirth of the Jewish People* (San Francisco: Harper and Row, 1983).
4. "The Netherlands: Manifesto of a Movement," *Christianity and Crisis*, September 21, 1981, 246-250.
5. Rosemary Ruether, *Women-Church: Theology and Practice of Feminist Liturgical Communities* (San Francisco: Harper and Row, 1986).
6. These remarks were made by Gregory Baum at a Conference on the Theology of the Church, Barat College, June, 1969.

Home delivery
from
Sheed & Ward

Here's your opportunity to have bestsellers delivered right to you. Our free catalog is filled with the newest titles on spirituality, church in the modern world, women in religion, ministry, small group resources, adult education/scripture, medical ethics videos and Sheed & Ward classics.

_____

Please send me a free Sheed & Ward catalog for home delivery.

NAME _____

ADDRESS _____

CITY _____ STATE/ZIP _____

If you have friends who would like to order books at home, we'll send them a catalog to —

NAME _____

ADDRESS _____

CITY _____ STATE/ZIP _____

NAME _____

ADDRESS _____

CITY _____ STATE/ZIP _____